# ISLAM AND THE UNITED STATES

GLEN R. COOK

Executive Press Ltd
Edmonton AB T6A 0H7
Canada
343-554-1210

Paperback ISBN:  979-8-9913174-4-3
Ebook ISBN:  979-8-9913174-5-0

# ISLAM
## And The
# UNITED STATES

GLEN R. COOK

Islam and the United States

What is the difference between a Religion and a political organization?

The difference is a religion is free choice. You can join or leave the religion; it is your choice. A political organization is not a free choice. The organization can force or coerce you to join as a matter of your survival. If you try to leave a political organization, it has the force of law. Depending on the organization, it may try to kill you.

# Contents

Do, you want to understand Afghanistan, huh?

What do Jimmy Carter's Iranian Embassy and Joe Biden's and Kamala Harris's loss of Afghanistan have in common? That's my first thought.

In both cases, the President saw the opposing government as an equal. Maintaining order was its dedication. The question never asked was who's order? One based on Greco-Roman standards for rights. Not hardly. Islamic Caliphates and Muslims aim to impose Sharia on all beliefs. Do the Taliban see an equal in Joe Biden or any other Washington president, except Obama? An equal, as in another Islamic. Or do they see a Christian? In other words, the Taliban sees an Infidel and any representative of the United States is an Infidel. Unless, of course, they are a Muslim. They scheme in private to overthrow the Constitution, enforcing Islamic code instead. If you worry about Muslims working against us, then consider this: Afghan soldiers we were training set ambushes and killed our people. How is this possible? Or could Muslims steal an Election to get an All Muslim Council in Hamtramck Michigan.?

Now would be a good time to look at the Moslem standard for integrity or truth. There are four words you should add to you lexicon:

**Notes**

The Hadith says Muslims can **lie** to unbelievers to defeat them or protect themselves. There are several forms. **Taqiyya** is one. It is saying something untrue about one's Muslim identity (i.e., whether one is a Muslim or what that means). This is a Shiite term: the Sunni counterpart is Muda'rat. **Kitman** - Lying by omission. An example is when Muslim apologists quote a fragment of verse 5:32. It says that if anyone kills «it will be as if he had killed all mankind.» They omit that the rest of the verse and the next verse mandate murder for undefined «corruption» and «mischief.»» **Tawriya** is a way to mislead. It states a true fact, leaving room for the listener's misinterpretation. This practice has a broader application than taqiyya. **Muruna** - ‹Blending in› by setting

4

aside some practices of Islam or Sharia to advance others. Though not called taqiyya, Muhammad clearly used deception. He signed a 10-year treaty with the Meccans (the Hudaibiya). It let him access their city while he secretly prepared to take over. He broke the treaty two years later. The unsuspecting residents were easily conquered. Some of the people in the city who had trusted him at his word were executed. Reference: Taqiyya: Deception and Lying in Islam (thereligionofpeace.com)

I would, also, recommend:

Why Muslim Friends Betray | Frontpagemag

'It Never Occurred to Us that Muslim Neighbors Would Betray Us...' – PJ Media

Now you understand how criminally naïve or subverted the State Department was.

Islamic countries view treaties as an opportunity to subvert an enemy or do a work around as Iran is doing in pursuit of the nuclear weapons. Quite successfully I might add. Back to Afghanistan, once President Biden gave the Taliban a timetable, the door was open to push the timetable forward. Also, those Islamics who worked with the Taliban now knew how long to wait before the Taliban would seek revenge, and what weapons they would get.

So, what was the United States trying to do in Afghanistan? In short, demuslify the country. BUT to do that it takes about fifty years. First, one MUST close all the Madrassahs and large Mosques. Second, you have to de-Islamize the school system. One step with this is to fully integrate the girls into the education system and classroom. Second step is to ban, like Qaddafi did in Libya, the hajib, and the burqa. Either everybody wears the same uniform or something similar. The third step is to teach the true history of Islam. It is one of greed, betrayal, murder, lies, and slavery. There are no Women's Rights or Science or Music and Art, and nothing positive. It will take at least two full generations before you can begin to hope for something decent or 50 or 60 years.

Another facet is the No-Go Zones. When Muslims build a mosque, they tend to gravitate to the neighborhood. This becomes a No-Go zone as Muslims do not respect infidel property rights. The No-Go Zone becomes an exclusive Muslim Economic Development Zone. The Muslims will gladly take any currency. But, they will avoid shopping in Infidel stores. The Muslims will force Restaurants to go Halal and raise Hell if something is Kosher.

The schools need to redo character building. They must explain, "Why was the Holocaust wrong?" and "What is genocide?" They should separate religion and science, and explain "Why separate religion and government?"

The lack of woman's rights causes several issues. First women are seen as property and have no right to the children they bear. The children are seen as property as well. See Organ Child Sale in this volume. Second, it is the cause of the sky-high suicide rate among Saudi women, a gilded cage if you will. The problem is so serious that a Qatari Princess fled her country for France. Another troubling aspect is the lack of paths to higher education and to spiritual and mental fulfilment. The Burqa and the Hajib strip woman of their identity and hyper-sexualize them leading to a rape culture. The lack of women's sports worsens medical issues, like China's foot binding decades ago. FGM, better known as Female Genital Mutilation, or the Hafud is another permanent medical problem that Islam forces on Women. Due to an Idiot Judge, it is now being performed in the United States where one state had tried to outlaw the practice. Remember, women not of your Islamic sect can be enslaved. They can be turned into sex slaves or baby factories (the Baby Jihad) due to Western welfare systems. Remember due to the Hafud, women cannot respond sexually to the physical act. The women in Afghanistan had a glimpse into a brighter future and our withdrawal changed all that and the woman are now back in the 700s.

Prayers five times a day is brainwashing 101. That practice needs to decease as well.

At the same time, until Islam is removed from being a predominant force, you cannot hope to have Democracy as a form of government. Islam is all about alpha males and power. Islam is not a religion, but a political system masquerading as a religion. It is way past time that Western and Eastern governments call a spade a Spade no matter how violent the followers get. The only way to stop the followers is to open their eyes. They must see the truth: Islam is a terror organization. Democracy requires every voice to be effective. When fifty percent are silenced (women), it does not reflect the people's will. I-Slam (what I call Islam) is all about the well-being of the Mullahs, Imams, Ayatollahs, and the other alpha males. Look at how the high-ranking Mullahs in Iran are prospering. Look at the relations in a family, especially concerning the father or Husband. Physical abuse is rampant, including the Hafud. You must remove the legal protection for family members who kill a female relative over "honor" violations. Hold the police and the courts accountable. No more whitewashing.

Biden's retreat undid whatever progress had been made and wasted 20 years. We will be in a continual state of war from now till the end of time because you can never tell when a Muslim will suddenly decide to become a Jihadi. The two countries that have solved the Muslim problem is Japan and Fiji. Both have banned Islam and do not grant Muslims citizenship.

# What Does Islam Teach About...
# Deception, Lying and Taqiyya

Does Islam permit Muslims to lie?

Muslim scholars teach that Muslims should be truthful to each other. The only exceptions are to "smooth over differences" or "gain the upper hand over an enemy.""

There are forms of lying to non-believers that are allowed in some cases. The best known is taqiyya (the Shia name). These are usually situations that help Islam. In some cases, they gain the trust of non-believers to exploit their vulnerability and defeat them.

Quran

Quran (16:106) - Establishes that there are circumstances that can "compel" a Muslim to tell a lie.

Quran (3:28) - This verse tells believers not to befriend non-Muslims, except to "guard themselves" against danger. This means a Muslim may seem friendly to non-Muslims, but should not feel friendly.

Quran (9:3) - "...Allah and His Messenger are free from liability to the idolaters..." The dissolution of oaths is with pagans who remained at Mecca following its capture. They did nothing wrong but were evicted anyway. (The next verse refers only to those who have a personal agreement with Muhammad as individuals - see Ibn Kathir vol 4, p 49)

Quran (66:2) - "Allah has already ordained for you the dissolution of your oaths..." Today's reader finds no specified circumstances for betraying your word. This leaves the verse open to interpretation. Yusuf Ali wrote in his commentary: "if your vows prevent you from doing good, or making peace, you should expiate the vow." (Presumably, whatever helps Islam counts as 'doing good').

Quran (40:28) - A man is introduced as a believer, but one who had to "hide his faith" among those who are not believers.

Quran (2:225) - "Allah will not call you to account for thoughtlessness in your oaths, but for the intention in your hearts" (see also 5:89)

Quran (3:54) - "And they (the disbelievers) schemed, and Allah schemed (against them): and Allah is the best of schemers." The Arabic word used here for scheme (or plot) is makara, which means 'cunning,' 'guile' and 'deceit'. If Allah is supremely deceitful toward unbelievers, then there is little basis for denying that Muslims are allowed to do the same. (See also 8:30 and 10:21)

These verses are interpreted to mean that, in some cases, a Muslim may be "compelled" to deceive others for a greater purpose.

Hadith and Sira

Sahih Bukhari (52:269) - "The Prophet said, 'War is deceit.'" It refers to the murder of Usayr ibn Zarim and his thirty unarmed companions by Muhammad's men after they were "guaranteed" safe passage (see More Notes below).

Sahih Bukhari (49:857) - "He who makes peace between the people by inventing good information or saying good things, is not a liar." In other words, lying is permissible when the end justifies the means.

Sahih Bukhari (84:64-65) - Ali, in power at the time, permits lying to deceive an "enemy."" The Quran defines the 'enemy' as "disbelievers" (4:101).

In Sahih Muslim (32:6303), he heard that exemption was not granted in anything that people speak as a lie, except in three cases: during battle, to bring reconciliation among individuals by relaying the words of a husband to his wife and vice versa (albeit twisted to reconcile them)."

Sahih Bukhari (50:369) - Recounts the murder of a poet, Ka'b bin al-Ashraf, at Muhammad's insistence. The men who volunteered for the assassination used lies to gain Ka'b's trust. They pretended to have turned against Muhammad. The victim emerged from his fortress, and then he was killed mercilessly.

From Islamic Law:

Reliance of the Traveler (p. 746 - 8.2) - "Speaking is a means to achieve objectives. If a worthy goal can be reached by both telling the truth and lying, it is wrong to lie. There is no need for it. If one can achieve a goal by lying but not by telling the truth, then it is permissible to lie if the goal is permissible. (In other words, the lie must bypass someone blocking a permissible action.) It is obligatory to lie if the goal is obligatory.. it is religiously precautionary in all cases to employ words that give a misleading impression... (See the Permissible Lying Section on the Sharia page for more)

"One should compare the bad results of lying to those of truth. If the truth is more damaging, one may lie.""

Notes

**The Hadith makes it clear that Muslims are allowed to lie to unbelievers in order to defeat them or protect themselves.** There are several forms:

Taqiyya - Saying something that isn't true as it relates to Muslim identity (i.e whether one is a Muslim or what that means). This is a Shiite term: the Sunni counterpart is Muda'rat.

Kitman - Lying by omission. An example is when Muslim apologists quote only part of verse 5:32. They cite that if anyone kills "it shall be as if he had killed all mankind." They neglect to mention that the rest of the verse (and the next) mandate murder for undefined cases of "corruption" and "mischief.""

Tawriya - It is to create a false impression by saying something true. It is done knowing the listener will interpret it differently. This practice has a broader application than taqiyya.

Muruna - 'Blending in' by setting aside some practices of Islam or Sharia in order to advance others.

Though not called taqiyya by name, Muhammad used deception. He signed a 10-year treaty with the Meccans (Hudaibiya). It allowed him access to their city while he secretly prepared to take over. The unsuspecting residents were easily conquered when he broke the treaty two years later. Some of the people in the city who had trusted him at his word were executed.

Another example of lying is when Muhammad used deception. He tricked his enemies into letting down their guard by pretending to seek peace. This happened in the case of Ka'b bin al-Ashraf (as noted). It also happened against Usayr ibn Zarim, a leader of the Banu Nadir. The Muslims had evicted the Banu Nadir from their home in Medina.

At the time, Usayr ibn Zarim was trying to raise an army against the Muslims. He sought support from a tribe allied with the Quraish, whom Muhammad had declared war on. Muhammad's "emissaries" went to ibn Zarim. They persuaded him to leave his safe haven to meet the prophet of Islam in Medina to discuss peace. The Muslims easily massacred the leader and his thirty companions. They were probably unarmed, as they had a guarantee of safe passage (Ibn Ishaq 981, Ibn Kathir v.4 p.300).

Such was the reputation of early Muslims for lying and killing that even those who "accepted Islam" did not feel entirely safe. Consider the fate of the Jadhima. When Muslim "missionaries" approached this tribe, one member insisted they would be slaughtered. They had "converted" to Islam to avoid such a fate. However, the others insisted they could trust the Muslim leader's promise. He said they would not be harmed if they offered no resistance. (After convincing the skeptic to lay down his arms, the unarmed men of the tribe were tied up and beheaded by the missionaries - Ibn Ishaq 834 & 837).

Today's apologists often excuse Muhammad's murder of his critics at Medina. They falsely claim the critics broke a treaty by their actions. Yet, these same apologists place little value on treaties broken by Muslims. From Muhammad to Saddam Hussein, promises to non-Muslims are non-binding in the Muslim mindset.

Arab world leaders sometimes say one thing in English, and a different thing in Arabic to their own people. Palestinian leaders tell Westerners of their desire for peace with Israel. Yet, they incite Palestinians to hate and attack Jews. Yassir Arafat openly referenced "Hudaibiya" - an admission to conning gullible non-Muslims.

The 9/11 hijackers practiced deception. They went into bars and drank alcohol to throw off any suspicion that they were fundamentalist jihadists. It worked so well that John Walsh, host of a popular TV show, claimed their bar trips were evidence of 'hypocrisy."

The Flight 93 transmission records the hijackers telling their doomed passengers that there is "a bomb on board." They said everyone would "be safe" if "their demands are met."" None of this was true, of course. But, these men were so devoted to Islam that they were willing to "slay and be slain for the cause of Allah" (as the Quran puts it). They saw nothing wrong with using taqiyya to aid their mission of mass murder.

The Islamic Society of North America (ISNA) insists it "has not now or ever been involved with the Muslim Brotherhood, or supported any covert, illegal, or terrorist activity or organization." In fact, it was created by the Muslim Brotherhood and has funded Hamas. At least nine founders or board members of ISNA have been accused by prosecutors of supporting terrorism.

The notorious Council on American Islamic Relations (CAIR) is known for lying about its ties to terror and extremism. Books have been written on the subject. They take seriously the part of Sharia that says, "it is permissible to lie if the goal is permissible and obligatory to lie if the goal is obligatory." The "goal" is the ascendency of Islam (and Sharia itself) on the American landscape.

In 2007, CAIR's Ibrahim Hooper published an op-ed with a fabricated story about Muhammad that portrayed him as a forgiving man:

There was a lady who threw garbage in the path of the prophet on a daily basis. One day, she didn 't do it. The prophet went to inquire about her health, because he thought she might be sick. This lady ended up converting to Islam. So, that 's how you respond to people who attack you, with forgiveness and with kindness.

Hooper is not ignorant. He knew what he was deceiving his audience. After getting caught, he changed it slightly. He now says it is a tradition "Muslims are taught." But, he still promotes the story without qualification. This causes others to unwittingly repeat a lie.

Before engineering deadly terror plots, like the Fort Hood massacre and a Detroit-bound airliner bombing attempt, American cleric Anwar al-Awlaki was often sought by NPR, PBS, and even government leaders to discuss Islam's peaceful nature.

In 2013, a scholar at al-Azhar university decreed that Muslims may wear the cross. It is to deceive Christians into thinking they are friendly. He cited 3:28 which says not to be friends with non-Muslims unless it is a way of "guarding" yourself against them.

"Hiding faith" can mean deceiving others about Islam in order to make it appear more attractive. For example, a prominent U.S. Muslim activist, Linda Sarsour, calls herself a "progressive." She says that gays, women, and religious minorities need not worry about Sharia being imposed. She even says that money is lent free of charge under Islamic law (more about that here).

In a 2020 video, Islamic apologist Zakir Naik said that Muslims should seem "kind" to critics of Islam in non-Muslim countries. But, they should arrest and punish them if they enter a Muslim-ruled land. In other words, the "kindness" is an act.

The Quran says in several places that Allah is the best at deceiving people.

Some early Quran verses encourage truthfulness: 70:32-33. Also, many Muslims are as honest as anyone else. But, when the Quran addresses lying, it is usually about the "lies against Allah." This refers to the Jews and Christians who rejected Muhammad's claim to be a prophet.

Muhammad allowed a believer to lie (to a non-spouse), but only in limited circumstances. They must either advance Islam or protect a Muslim from harm. While this is vital for global security, like with Iran's nuclear plans, it does not justify distrust of any Muslim one might meet on the street or at work.

Additional Reading:
Taqiyya: TROP's Response to the Apologists
Taqiyya about Taqiyya (Raymond Ibrahim)
Knowing the Four Forms of Lying
Muruna: Violating Sharia to Fool the West
What is Taqiyya? (David Wood Video)
©2002 - 2021 Site developed by TheReligionofPeace.Com
*Daruriyyat, Hajiyyat and Tahsiniyyat*

# Classification of Maqasid Syariah - The daruriyyat, the hajiyyat and the tahsiniyyat.

Muslim scholars classify maqasid-cum-masalih into three categories, in order of importance: the daruriyyat (the essential), the hajiyyat (the complementary), and the tahsiniyyat (the desirable).

The essential masalih are enumerated as five: life, faith, intellect, lineage, and property. These are vital for individuals' survival and spiritual well-being. Their destruction would cause chaos and the end of social order.

The Shari'ah seeks to protect and promote these values. It validates all measures to preserve and advance them. Theft, adultery, and drinking alcohol are punishable offences. They threaten private property, the family, and the mind, respectively.

In a positive way, but at a different level, the Shari'ah encourages work and trade. It aims to help individuals earn a living. It also sets rules to ensure smooth commercial transactions in the marketplace.

The Shari'ah encourages the pursuit of knowledge and education. It aims to develop the people and advance the arts, sciences, and civilization. The essential masalih, in other words, are the Shari'ah's core theme. All its laws aim to protect these benefits.

The second category of benefits, called the hajiyyah, or the complimentary benefits, seeks to remove hardship. This applies only when the hardship does not threaten the survival of normal order.

Most rukhas (concessions), like shortening the salah and forgoing the fast, are hajiyyah. They apply to the sick or travelers. In almost all areas of obligatory 'ibadah, the Shari'ah has granted such concessions. These concessions aim to prevent hardship. They allow a reduction of an obligation or a temporary inability to perform it.

The third category of masalih, called the tahsiniyyah, is about desirabilities. It seeks to refine and perfect people's customs and conduct. The Shari'ah encourages a clean body and attire for 'ibadah. It recommends wearing perfume when attending the Friday prayer.

The Shari'ah also encourages the giving of charity to those in need, over and above the obligatory charity (zakat). Again, in the area of 'ibadah, it recommends supererogatory prayers and voluntary fasting. The Shari'ah, in customs and relationships, encourages al-rifq (gentleness), husn al-khulq (pleasant speech and conduct), and ihsan (fair dealing).

In criminal law, there is a desire to lessen harshness. So, the judge and the head of state are advised not to be too eager to enforce penalties. If there is any doubt about guilt, a lesser punishment is preferable. This is shown in a hadith related by Al-Hakim and As-Suyuti: "Refrain from enforcing hudud on Muslims as much as you can."

If you find a way out for a Muslim, let him (or her) go, as it is better for the imam (ruler) to wrongly forgive than to wrongly punish." Being too eager or severe in meting out punishment is thus considered to be undesirable. The purpose of all this is the attainment of refinement and excellence in all areas of human conduct.

The tahsiniyyah are a very important category, as they are all-pervasive and relate to all the other masalih. One can perform the obligatory salah, for example, with full concentration. One can also perform it with haste and thoughtlessness.

The two ends of the spectrum differ. At one end, the individual performing the salah aims to attain both the essential and the desirable.

They want to fulfill a duty while reaping the greatest spiritual benefit. At the other end, it is just a perfunctory discharging of duty. One can extend this analysis to the implementation of almost all the ahkam of the Shari'ah, and indeed, to almost every area of human conduct.

Maqasid (Higher Objectives) of Shari'ah
By Dr. Mohammad Hashim Kamali

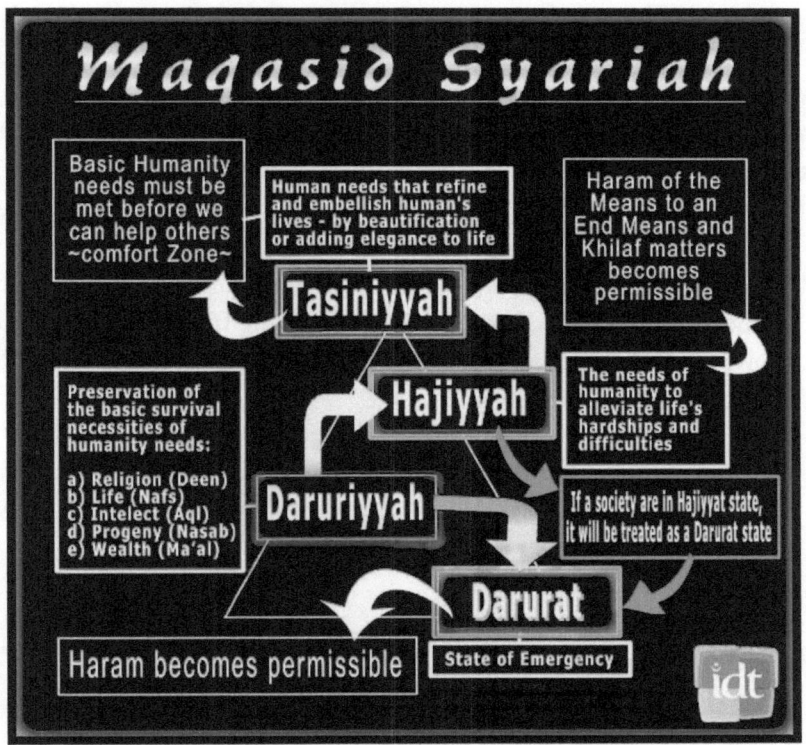

Daruriyyah is the basic necessity for welfare. It includes:
Protection of Faith
Protection of Life
Protection of Wisdom
Protection of Progeny
Protection of Property

If the state of Daruriyyah were not met, then humanity would fall into Darurat. This is when this basic necessities (daruriyyat) ceases to exist, or in other word...Darurah is a declaration of state of emergency. This is where Qawaid al Fiqhiyyah Maxim #3 'Hardship begets facility' (ref: http://ilmuislamuallaf.blogspot.my/2014/12/qawaid-al-fiqhiyyah-legal-maxim-no-3.html) and Maxim #4 'Harm or Hardship must be Eliminated' kicks in (ref: http://ilmuislamuallaf.blogspot.my/2014/12/qawaid-al-fiqhiyyah-legal-maxim-no-4.html). This is where the End Means and Khilaf (matters of differing opinions) become Mubah or even Fardh/Wajib. If life could be saved, it's allowed to perform a prohibition, like eating pork when starving or drinking alcohol while choking. Daruriyyah is the fundamental to hajiyyah and hajiyyah is the foundation of tahsiniyyah. In other words, tahsiniyyah (beautification) is the complement of hajiyyah (requirements). Hajiyyah is the complement of daruriyyah (necessities). If humanity's basic needs (daruriyyah) are unmet, it falls into a 'state of emergency' or Darurat. If Daruriyyat state is not met, humanity will be in Darurat situation. If Hajiyyat is not met, humanity will be in Hajat situation. If a Society is in Hajiyyat state, it will be treated ar a Darurat state.

# Taqiyya: Iran Actually Boasts About Deceiving the West in Nuclear Talks

by <u>Raymond Ibrahim</u> June 9, 2023, at 5:00 am

Iran's Supreme Guide, Ayatollah Ali Khamenei "used the Islamic concept of 'Taqiyya' to describe the regime's decision to accept the 2015 JCPOA nuclear deal with the West. Taqiyya means the permissibility to deny or conceal one's real beliefs to secure a worthy goal." Pictured: Khamenei (R) speaks with Islamic Revolutionary Guard Corps general Ali Akbar Ahmadian (2nd L) in an undisclosed location, in an undated photo released on May 22, 2023. (Photo by khamenei.ir/AFP via Getty Images)

Iran's Supreme Guide, Ayatollah Ali Khamenei "used the Islamic concept of 'Taqiyya' to describe the regime's decision to accept the 2015 JCPOA nuclear deal with the West. Taqiyya means the permissibility to deny or conceal one's real beliefs to secure a worthy goal." — iranintl. com, May 20, 2023.

"Khamenei's emphasis on "expediency" as the third principle in foreign policy was notable. He urged flexibility "in necessary instances" and to bypass "tough barriers" to stay the course."" — iranintl.com, May 20, 2023

If it was not clear what "heroic flexibility" meant then, it probably should be clear by now. Reports consistently document that Iran has been cheating since day one.

"[Khamenei] said that when a revolution hits a tough rock on its path, it need not break its head against it; the wisest course would be to try and go around it." — Amir Taheri, "Iran: Heroic Flexibility Returns," June 4, 2023.

" [A]l- Taqiyya is with the tongue only, (not the heart)." — Jalal al-Din al-Suyuti in his book, "al-Durr al-Manthoor Fi al-Tafsir al-Ma'athoor," quoting Ibn Abbas.

Taqiyya is actually all around us. Iran pretends that its nuclear program is just for peaceful purposes. Some Muslims, both past and present, pretend to convert to Christianity. A Muslim gunman gained entry to a church by feigning interest in Christian prayers.

It should not be surprising, therefore, that Khamenei is relying on taqiyya once again. What is surprising is that the Biden Administration is falling for it. They were warned it would be used. Now, they are either being sucker-punched or pretending to allow it.

In 1994, PLO leader Yasser Arafat signed the Oslo Accord with Israel. He justified his actions, saying, "This agreement is no more than the one signed between our Prophet Muhammad and the Quraysh in Mecca." This referred to a truce, the Treaty of Hudaibiyah. Muhammad broke it as soon as he regained power and could attack.

Khamenei is signaling, by citing taqiyya in Iran's nuclear deal with the West, that Iran is only going along for "expediency." It will betray the deal once it can pursue its nuclear goals.

[I]s there a single authority representing the West at these international nuclear talks that knows — let alone cares about — any of this? Or is the fix already in?

The Islamic doctrine of "taqiyya," or dissimulation, is back in the news. It permits Muslims to deceive non-Muslims to advance Islam. In a speech delivered on May 20, 2023, Iran's Supreme Guide, Ayatollah Ali Khamenei, according to a report,

"Explain and clarify the principles of 'a successful foreign policy.' Focus on three keywords: Honor, wisdom, and expediency."

"Khamenei... used the Islamic concept of 'Taqiyya' to describe the regime's decision to accept the 2015 JCPOA nuclear deal with the West. Taqiyya means the permissibility to deny or conceal one's real beliefs to secure a worthy goal...."

Khamenei's emphasis on "expediency" as the third principle in foreign policy was notable. He urged flexibility "in necessary instances" and to bypass "tough barriers" to stay the course.

His mention of "flexibility" referred to his phrase, "heroic flexibility." In 2013, he used it to permit the start of nuclear talks.

If it was not clear what "heroic flexibility" meant then, it probably should be clear by now. Reports show that Iran has been cheating since day one (here, here, and here). They allege that the IAEA has been hoodwinked and has "capitulat[ed] to Iranian pressure.'"

This week, the Iranian scholar Amir Taheri wrote, "Iran: Heroic Flexibility Returns." He is a former editor of Iran's top newspaper, Kayhan.

"[Khamenei] has decided to perform what he calls 'heroic flexibility' in foreign policy.... In a speech last week, he said he was applying the tactic of 'taqiyeh' (dissimulation), a theological concept, to diplomacy.... [H]e said that when a revolution hits a tough rock on its path, it need not break its head against it; the wisest course would be to try and go around it.

"Against that, Tehran now hails its recent 'normalization' with Saudi Arabia. It also welcomes 'dispersing the clouds' in relations with the UAE. It calls these moves 'a major step towards Islamic solidarity.'"

Taqiyya is a key doctrine that Westerners often overlook in their dealings with Muslims. In short, it allows Muslims to do anything. This includes cursing Muhammad and being baptized. As long as they stay committed Muslims at heart, their deception must benefit themselves or Islam.

Jalal al-Din al-Suyuti's book, "al-Durr al-Manthoor Fi al-Tafsir al-Ma'athoor," cites Ibn Abbas. It says, "Al-Taqiyya is with the tongue only, (not the heart)." (For copious documentation, see here).

Taqiyya is actually all around us. Iran pretends that its nuclear program is just for peaceful purposes. Some Muslims pretend to convert to Christianity, both now and in the past. Or, a Muslim gunman gains entry to a church by feigning interest in Christian prayers. Examples abound.

It should not be surprising, therefore, that Khamenei is relying on taqiyya once again. What is surprising is that the Biden Administration is falling for it. They were warned it would be used. Now, they are either being sucker-punched or pretending to allow it.

Taqiyya permeates all Muslim politics. According to the late Sami Mukaram, the world's leading authority on taqiyya:

"Taqiyya is of fundamental importance in Islam. Practically every Islamic sect agrees to it and practices it... We can go so far as to say that the practice of taqiyya is mainstream in Islam, and that those few sects not practicing it diverge from the mainstream... Taqiyya is very prevalent in Islamic politics, especially in the modern era." (Mukaram, Sami, *At-Taqiyya fi 'l-Islam*, London: Mu'assisat at-Turath ad-Druzi, 2004, p. 7; author's translation)

The earliest records of Islam attest to the prevalence of taqiyya — deception and betrayal. This is still a legal strategy for Muslims against non-Muslims, especially the infidel. It includes lying, if it's justified as a form of jihad to empower Islam or Muslims, even through nuclear weapons. In the long wars with Christians, wherever they were in power, taqiyya became more common.

Also, early Islamic texts often depict early Muslims as lying to escape difficult situations. They would usually deny or insult Islam or Muhammad. Often, this pleased him. The only criterion was that their intentions (niya) be pure. [Mukaram, *At-Taqiyya fi 'l-Islam*, pp. 11-2.]

Professor Mukaram states:

"Taqiyya was a way to fend off danger from the Muslims. It was used in critical times when their borders were exposed to wars with the Byzantines and later, to raids by the Franks and others. [Mukaram, At-Taqiyya fi 'l-Islam, pp. 41-42]

The Spanish Inquisition was prompted by the widespread use of taqiyya. Hundreds of thousands of Muslims, who pretended to convert to Christianity, conspired with North African Muslim tribes to reconquer the Iberian Peninsula. [Devin Stewart, "Islam in Spain after the Reconquista," Emory University, p. 2, accessed Nov. 27, 2009.]

Although many scholars associate taqiyya with the Shia branch of Islam (the sort practiced in Iran), that is not entirely true. In 1994, PLO leader Yasser Arafat signed the Oslo Accord with Israel. Fellow Arabs criticized him for conceding too much. He justified his actions by saying, "This agreement is no more than the one signed between our Prophet Muhammad and the Quraysh in Mecca." He meant the Treaty of Hudaibiyah, a truce that Muhammad broke after he regained power and could attack.

As a persecuted minority among their Sunni rivals, the Shias have often had more reason to perfect the art of dissembling. This was to save themselves from the Sunnis (ISIS, al-Qaeda, Al Shabaab, Boko Haram, and Hamas are all Sunni).

Khamenei, by citing taqiyya in Iran's nuclear deal with the West, is signaling that Iran is only going along for "expediency" – as he stated above. It will renege once it can pursue its nuclear aims.

In short, as this author has noted:

23

The prophet of Islam, Muhammad... regularly made use of deceit. In order to assassinate a poet (Ka'b ibn Ashraf) who offended him, Muhammad permitted a Muslim to lie to the poet. Muhammad is on record permitting breaking oaths for a better offer. He allowed lying, without tawriya, to one's wife and in war. As for the latter, it assumes a perpetual jihad to make Islam supreme (e.g., Qur'an 8:39). In that case, deception and lies are permissible.

That said, is there a single authority representing the West at these nuclear talks that knows — let alone cares — about any of this? Or is the fix already in?

Raymond Ibrahim, author of Defenders of the West and Sword and Scimitar, is a fellow at two institutes. He is the Distinguished Senior Shillman Fellow at the Gatestone Institute. He is also the Judith Rosen Friedman Fellow at the Middle East Forum.

# When–and Why–Muslim Friends Betray

**08/04/2019 by Raymond Ibrahim FrontPage Magazine**

Arabic media reported on a troubling aspect of the recent gang-rape and murder of a 60-year-old Christian teacher in Syria. It was as follows (in translation):

Her rapists and murderers are from the [jihadi] organization, al-Nusra. Some of them are foreigners but others are from the area. In other words, her rapists and murderers are her former students and neighbors. She taught them Arabic in school for 30 years. Surely she never dreamt to see such depraved savagery in the eyes of her former students…. Nonetheless, they preyed on her like wild beasts—even though wild beasts do not rape their mothers (emphasis added).

**The third category of Muslims lurks between "moderates" and "radicals": "Sleepers." They seem "moderate," but turn "radical" when the time is right. After ISIS entered the Syrian city of Hassakè, it caused a mass exodus of Christians. Many otherwise "normal" Muslims joined ISIS and turned on their Christian neighbors.**

**This shift has played out countless times over whenever and wherever Islamic terror groups infiltrate.** These are testimonials from non-Muslims, mostly Christian refugees from Iraq and Syria. They fled areas under ISIS or other jihadi control. Consider what they say about their longtime Muslim neighbors. They seemed "moderate" or at least nonviolent. But, when the jihad came to town, their true colors showed.

Georgios, from the ancient Christian town of Ma'loula, Syria, tells of how his lifelong Muslim neighbors turned once al-Nusra. That jihadi outfit gang-raped and murdered 60-year-old Christian women. They invaded in 2013.

We knew our Muslim neighbours all our lives. Yes, we knew the Diab family were quite radical, but we thought they would never betray us. We ate with them. We are one people. A few of the Diab family had left months ago and we guessed they were with the Nusra. But their wives and children were still here. We looked after them. Then, two days before the Nusra attacked, the families suddenly left the town. We didn't know why. And then our neighbours led our enemies in among us (emphasis added).

After explaining how he saw a young Diab family member, whom he knew from youth, holding a sword and leading foreign jihadis to Christian homes, Georgios continues:

We had excellent relations. It never occurred to us that Muslim neighbours would betray us. We all said "please let this town live in peace — we don't have to kill each other." But now there is bad blood. They brought in the Nusra to throw out the Christians and get rid of us forever. Some of the Muslims who lived with us are good people, but I will never trust 90 per cent of them again.

A teenage Christian girl from Homs, Syria, relates her story:

We left because they were trying to kill us. . ... They wanted to kill us because we were Christians. They were calling us Kaffirs [infidels], even little children saying these things. Those who were our neighbors turned against us. At the end, when we ran away, we went through balconies. We did not even dare go out on the street in front of our house. I've kept in touch with the few Christian friends left back home, but I cannot speak to my Muslim friends anymore. I feel very sorry about that. (Crucified Again, p. 207; emphasis added).

An anonymous Christian refugee explained, when asked, who drove Christians out of Mosul, Iraq.

We left Mosul because ISIS came to the city. The [Sunni Muslim] people of Mosul embraced ISIS and drove the Christians out of the city. When ISIS entered Mosul, the people hailed them and drove out the Christians.... The people who embraced ISIS, the people who lived there with us... Yes, my neighbors. Our neighbors and other people threatened us. They said: "Leave before ISIS get you." What does that mean? Where would we go? ... Christians have no support in Iraq (emphasis added).

Other "infidels," Yazidis for example, have experienced the same betrayal. Discussing the ISIS invasion of his village, a 68-year-old Yazidi man said:

**The (non-Iraqi) jihadists were Afghans, Bosnians, Arabs and even Americans and British fighters.... But the worst killings came from the people living among us, our (Sunni) Muslim neighbours.... The Metwet, Khawata and Kejala tribes—they were all our neighbours. But they joined the IS, took heavy weapons from them, and informed on who was Yazidi and who was not. Our neighbours made the IS takeover possible (emphasis added).**

In an interview, a Yazidi woman was asked why her lifelong friends suddenly joined ISIS and turned on her people. She replied:

I can't tell you exactly, but it has to be religion. It has to be religion. They constantly asked us to convert, but we refused. Before this, they never mentioned it. Prior, we thought of each other as family. But I say, it has to be religion (emphasis added).

**This phenomenon is not limited to the Islamic State in Syria and Iraq. In Nigeria, a nation with little in common with Syria and Iraq, except for its Islam, a jihadi attack destroyed five churches and killed several Christians. "Local Muslims," who were once friendly with the Christians, enabled the attack.**

This phenomenon is not linked to any modern Muslim "grievances." These include the existence of Israel, "blasphemous" cartoons, and a "lack of job opportunities." Western talking heads often cite these to rationalize Muslim hatred. The following anecdote, over one century old and from the Ottoman Empire, speaks for itself:

Then one night, my husband came home. He said the padisha [sultan] had ordered us to kill all the Christians in our village. We would have to kill our neighbours. I was very angry and told him that I did not care who gave such orders, they were wrong. These neighbours had always been kind to us. But, he killed them — with his own hand. (Sir Edwin Pears, Turkey and Its People, London: Methuen and Co., 1911, p. 39; emphasis added).

This, then, is the other, forgotten group of Muslims. They lurk between "moderates" and "radicals": sleepers, whose loyalty can shift at any moment.

# It Never Occurred to Us that Muslim Neighbors Would Betray Us...':

### The Call to Jihad Can Override All Existing Loyalties.
### October 1, 2013

Ideally, a neighborhood is a small family. It's a community of kind, sympathetic people. They share local interests, despite their differences. The family in Islamic law is a community of a man and his slaves, not a loving bond between a man and a woman. Likewise, Islamic supremacists don't envision a friendly neighborhood. You can't chat with your neighbor over the fence.

We have seen illustrated anew in Syria recently, as Robert Fisk (of all people!) reported last week in the Independent: "The Diab family," Fisk wrote, "can never return to Maaloula. "Not since the Christians of this beautiful, sacred town saw their Muslim neighbors leading armed Nusrah Islamists to their homes.""

"We knew our Muslim neighbors all our lives," says one Christian whose home was destroyed. "Yes, we knew the Diab family were quite radical, but we thought they would never betray us. We ate with them. We are one people."

The Christians, he said, had even looked after the wives and children of local jihad fighters while they were away:

A few of the Diab family had left months ago and we guessed they were with the Nusra. But their wives and children were still here. We looked after them. Then, two days before the Nusra attacked, the families suddenly left the town. We didn't know why. And then our neighbours led our enemies in among us.

This was an ugly shock, because previously "there was a kind of coexistence between us. We had excellent relations. It never occurred to us that Muslim neighbors would betray us. We all said, 'please let this town live in peace – we don't have to kill each other'. But now there is bad blood. They brought in the Nusra to throw out the Christians and get rid of us forever. Some of the Muslims who lived with us are good people, but I will never trust 90 percent of them again."

Their Muslim friends and neighbors turned on the unbelievers and killed them – and this was not a singular occurrence. The June 19, 2013, New York Times had a photo of a woman, Ibtisam Ali Aboud. The caption said, "her husband, a Syrian Alawite, was killed by his Sunni friend." It showed how the call to jihad can override all loyalties, even a friendship between an Alawite and a Sunni. There are many other examples. One is Boston Marathon jihad bomber Tamerlan Tsarnaev. He apparently murdered his Jewish "best friend" by slitting his throat on September 11, 2011.

Similarly, on August 6, 2003, in Houston, a Muslim named Mohammed Ali Alayed slashed the throat of his friend Ariel Sellouk, who was Jewish. Alayed had broken off his friendship with Sellouk when he began to become more devout in his Islam. On the night of the murder, Alayed called Sellouk. They went to a bar, then back to Alayed's apartment. There, Alayed slit Sellouk's throat, nearly beheading him. The two were not seen arguing at the bar. Alayed killed Sellouk in a style of jihadist murder in Iraq. He then went to a mosque. Authorities said they found no evidence that Sellouk was killed because of his race or religion."

But there wasn't anything else that explained why he was killed, and in light of Alayed's religious awakening, it could not be discounted. However, authorities most likely were unaware of a phenomenon.

Muslims were suddenly turning on longtime non-Muslim friends and killing them. Yet it was nothing new. Fisk notes that "twenty years ago, identical tragedies destroyed the villages of Bosnia. Now they are being re-enacted in Syria."

And it goes back longer than that as well. An anecdote from the Ottoman Empire in the late nineteenth century:

Then one night, my husband came home. He said the padisha had ordered us to kill all the Christians in our village, including our neighbors. I was very angry and told him that I did not care who gave such orders, they were wrong. These neighbours had always been kind to us, and if he dared to kill them Allah would pay us out. I tried all I could to stop him, but he killed them — killed them with his own hand. (Sir Edwin Pears, Turkey and Its People, London: Methuen and Co., 1911, p. 39)

Discussing cases of Muslims betraying their non-Muslim friends is "Islamophobia." It implies all Muslims will eventually turn on their non-Muslim friends. Islamic spokesmen in the U.S. falsely claim that anyone who opposes jihad terror is attacking all Muslims.

However, to remain silent about it would be to double the betrayal of the Christians of Maaloula. They found, to their sorrow, that Muslims attacking their Christian friends was real, not "bigotry." They deserve support. We must honestly discuss what happened in Maaloula. Both Muslims and non-Muslims must find ways to prevent it from happening again. But if anything is in short supply in the public discourse these days, it is honesty.

By Robert Spencer Source
Recent Posts
Islam: The Facade and the Facts
America's Values Can Contribute to Its Vulnerability
'It Never Occurred to Us that Muslim Neighbours Would Betray Us...': The Call to Jihad Can Override All Existing Loyalties.
After Kenya, no more turning the other cheek to those who hate us.
Obama-linked Islamists Downplay Coptic Suffering on social media

# "I am not American," said the Islamist; "I am Muslim."

**by Majid Rafizadeh December 2, 2017, at 5:00 am**

For Islamists, non-Muslim land is different from Muslim land. Many cannot identify with a Western land, flag, or nationality. This is true even if they were born there and their families lived there for generations.

Brainwashing people to reject a flag and a nationality harms community ties. It hurts communication. It pits the indoctrinated person against the entire society and his own countrymen and develops an "us versus them" mentality.

This view brings with it a wish for waging jihad against one's birth country. It creates the priority -- if the country attacking it is ruled by shari'ah -- of joining the enemy to fight against one's birth country.

Several years ago, when first in the United States on a teaching scholarship, one issue leapt out. A man asked an innocent enough question: Where I was from? I told him; then, as a courtesy, asked him the same question.

"I am a Muslim," he smiled.

Thinking that perhaps he had not understood the question -- he sounded American or English -- I asked if he was from the United States.

"I am not American," he said again; "I am a Muslim."

I later learned he was an Islamist, a strict religious preacher. Many of his followers shared his views.

In Iran and Syria, where I was born and raised, I had never before heard this answer.

Later, while speaking in Europe, these notions kept resurfacing. Radical Islamists, particularly in Britain and France, proclaim themselves first to be Muslim. Even when they speak with English, French or American accents, they do not name their countries -- even to me, someone from the Middle East.

Their response signals a reason for concern in the countries they live in now. To begin with, for Islamists, non-Muslim land is different from Muslim land. Many cannot identify with a Western land, a flag, or a nationality. They may have been born there, and their families lived there for generations.

This view is far different from that in the Middle East.

One day, I asked an American imam why he did not identify himself as an American. Millions of people, I said to him, dream of coming to the US and becoming Americans; why would anyone want to reject this?

He quoted said one of the founding fathers of Islamist thoughts, Sayyid Qutb:

"The homeland of the Muslim is not a piece of land. It is what he lives in and defends. His nationality is not that of any government. It is how he is identified. The family of the Muslim is not just blood relatives. It is where he finds solace and for which he fights. The flag of the Muslim is not a country's flag. It is what he honors and under which he is martyred. The victory of the Muslim is not a military win. It is what he celebrates and for which he thanks God.'"

I realized that Western Islamists were stricter and more fundamentalist than the Middle Eastern Islamists I had grown up with. Once, in a casual chat with an American Islamist preacher and his followers, I mentioned the name of a deceased imam. I forgot to add a religious praise, like "Allah's peace be upon him."" There was a chill. The conversation came to a halt. The American Islamist preacher and his followers did not hesitate to express their anger.

You see that, when people are brainwashed not to identify with a flag and a nationality, it disrupts the human connections in communities. It pits the indoctrinated person against the entire society and his own countrymen and develops an "us versus them" mentality. The indoctrinated group then wants to create its own group. For Islamists, it is an ummah (borderless Islamic community). Emotion and sympathy for fellow countrymen disappear. People feel isolated from other citizens and see themselves as separate. Respect for the social order and the laws of the land vanish, as Islamic laws become more vital, and obedience is then just to shari'ah.

Islamist teachings in the West seem to focus on indoctrination. They aim to make followers identify with Islamist ideals, not with a nationality. Islamist beliefs should come before all else, even family and friends.

The teachings of these Islamist preachers further echo what Sayed Qutb said:

"A Muslim's only bond with his family is through [Allah]. They are also connected by blood." A Muslim has no country but where God's Shari'ah is law. There, human ties are based on a relationship with God. A Muslim has no nationality but his belief. It makes him part of the Muslim community in Dar-ul-Islam. A Muslim's only relatives are those who believe in God. This belief bonds him with other Believers."

Do these Western Islamists then ever identify themselves with their land and flag? Not, according to their teachings, until the law of the land is shari'ah. As Syed Qutb also stated:

"The fatherland is where the Islamic faith and Shari'ah of God are dominant. Only this meaning of 'fatherland' is worthy of humans." There is only one place on earth that is the home of Islam (Dar-ul-Islam). It is where the Islamic state is established, the Shari'ah is the authority, and God's limits are observed. There, all Muslims run the state with mutual consultation. The rest of the world is the home of hostility (Dar-ul-Harb). A Muslim can have only two possible relations with Dar-ul-Harb: peace with a contractual agreement, or war. A country with which there is a treaty will not be considered the home of Islam."

This view brings with it a wish for waging jihad (war in the cause of Islam) against one's birth country. It creates the priority -- if the country attacking it is ruled by shari'ah -- of joining the enemy to fight against one's birth country.

"The honor of martyrdom is achieved only when one is fighting in the cause of God, and if one is killed for any other purpose, this honor will not be attained."

Brainwashing people to reject their flag and nationality harms community connections and communications. It pits the indoctrinated person against the entire society and his own countrymen and develops an "us versus them" mentality. Pictured: Muslims demonstrate in Sydney, Australia, September 15, 2012. (Image source: Jamie Kennedy/ Flickr)

Western governments must address extreme Islamist beliefs. They have serious social, political, and security implications. These beliefs disrupt the social order, peace, and human rights. If allowed to continue, these beliefs will become more rampant, and the consequences more severe.

Dr. Majid Rafizadeh is a business advisor and a Harvard-educated scholar. He is a political scientist. He is a board member of the Harvard International Review. He is also the president of the International American Council on the Middle East. He is the author of "Peaceful Reformation in Iran's Islam". He can be reached at Dr.Rafizadeh@Post.Harvard.Edu.

Follow Majid Rafizadeh on Twitter

# Reality is Citizenship Analysis

Given what we know about Muslim lying, a Muslim's citizenship in any non-Islamic country is a threat to both Western and Eastern cultures. It is to overthrow any existing culture or laws. They want to replace them with Sharia, and all the horrors of Islam, including genocide, murder, and slavery.

The truth be told, it comes down to a hard choice. Do we sanction and allow Islam of Any and ALL sorts to the detriment of all other Religions or do we defend the Constitution?

The Answer has to be we defend the Constitution, with no ends, if, or buts about the Constitution.

Islam. By its very nature calls for the Genocide of ALL other Religions.
Look at the attacks on Jews in Israel.
Look at the attacks on Hindus in India,
Look at the attacks on Jews, Christians, and Churches in Europe. er
Look at the escalating attacks in the UNITED STATES.

Do you see a pattern here? You should.
No Muslim can honestly swear to support and defend the Constitution when Sharia is directly in conflict with Sharia. No Muslim can swear allegiance to any government that is not Sharia and mean it.

Furthermore, for this same reason of lying and telling the Truth, Muslims should not be allowed to hold any office in government.

How many times do we have to have a Muslim commit a violent act only to get released on bail or parole and flee to a home Muslim Country. Sirhan Sirhan received a warm reception upon returning to Lebanon. He killed Robert Kennedy during a Presidential campaign, if you don't remember. Sirhan returned a HERO.

At the same time, until Islam is removed from being a predominant force, you cannot hope to have Democracy as a form of government. Islam is all about alpha males and power. Islam is not a religion, but a political system masquerading as a religion. Democracy requires every voice to be effective. When fifty percent are silenced (women), it doesn't reflect the people's will. I-Slam (what I call Islam) is all about the well-being of the Mullahs, Imams, Ayatollahs, and the other ALPHA males. Look at how the high-ranking Mullahs in Iran are prospering. Look at the relations in a family, especially concerning the father or Husband. Physical abuse is rampant, including the Hafud. You must remove the legal protection for family members who kill a female relative over "honor" violations. Hold the police and the courts accountable. No more whitewash.

Biden's retreat undid whatever progress had been made and wasted 20 years. To demulsify a country and have a hope of success will take at least 40 years at the very minimum. To fully complete the DeMuslification will take at least 60 to 70 years. Remember in ancient times, you were not allowed to claim citizenship unless you had lived in a kingdom for at least three generations. The same should hold true today, especially in the United States. Some U.S. Congress members and their descendants are trying to sabotage the Constitution. They are immigrants. Members Tlaib and Ilhan being a case in point. We will be in a continual state of war from now till the end of time because you can never tell when a Muslim will suddenly decide to become a Jihadi. The two countries that have solved the Muslim problem is Japan and Fiji. Both have banned Islam and do not grant Muslims citizenship. The United States should strip Moslems of citizenship, period. It is not fair, but it is justified and just.

Truth be told, anyone, from Congressman to President, should be removed from office for supporting Islam. Islam is the antithesis of our Constitution, democracy, and capitalism.

For reference I give you: "I am not American," said the Islamist; "I am Muslim" by Majid Rafizadeh December 2, 2017 at 5:00 am from Gatestone Institute. Also, in the beginning of this tome.

# Islamic Slavery and Racism

**April 2, 2013 By** <u>Daniel Greenfield</u>

When Tuaregs and Islamists swarmed in to seize Northern Mali, one of the old grievances animating their campaign was slavery. The Tuaregs were not former slaves, they were, and in some cases still are, slaveholders.

The French invasion of Northern Mali liberated towns from Islamist rule. It echoed the original French emancipation of Tuareg slaves in the colonial period. Despite French efforts, the Tuareg tried to keep their slaves. Muslim Tuareg still hold thousands of slaves in Northern Mali.

Mali is not unique. The Sudanese genocide was fueled by a belief. Arabs and Muslims had a natural right to be superior to African Animists and Christians. Today, Omar Hassan al-Bashir, the Butcher of Sudan, is still supported by the Muslim world. This is despite his indictment for genocide by the International Criminal Court.

Supporters of the Muslim world's drive to replace Israel's Jews with Arab colonists casually accuse Israel of apartheid. Every year, Israeli Apartheid Week is held on college campuses. It tries to compare Israel's refusal to let Hamas into its territory with racial discrimination.

But racial Apartheid is very much a reality in the Muslim world. The same Muslim students who denounce Israel as an apartheid state often come from countries with true apartheid against black people.

In North Africa, the Haratin, a Berber word meaning dark skin, are the remnants of the indigenous African population. Many are still enslaved. Others live apart from mainstream society, forced into degrading or difficult occupations.

Mauritania is the country with the world's largest proportion of slaves. There hundreds of thousands of Haratin serve the Bidhan, the so-called "White Moors". The Bidhan pass on the Haratin as property from generation to generation. And even those who are not legally property face a grim life.

In the 80s, Mauritania ethnically cleansed tens of thousands of Africans from its territory. Even Human Rights Watch stated, "It is fair to say that the Mauritanian government practices undeclared apartheid and severely discriminates on the basis of race."

The best kept secrets of the Muslim world include large populations of former African slaves in places like Pakistan, Iraq and Turkey. Africans in Israel are not descended from slaves. But, Afro-Arabs, Afro-Turks, and African Pakistanis are reminders of a Muslim slave trade that sometimes still lingers on.

The world's greatest slave rebellion was in Basra, Iraq. There, half a million African slaves rose against the Arab Abbasid Empire.

The Zanj rebellion was brutally suppressed. Its legacy lives on in Basra, where hundreds of thousands of despised Afro-Iraqis are taunted with the slur "Abd," or "Slave." That same Arabic word is often widely applied to black people in the Middle East.

Muslim propagandists have used the legacy of U.S. slavery to win black converts. But, slavery in the Muslim world began long before the U.S. and ended a century later.

President Abraham Lincoln issued the Emancipation Proclamation in 1862. By contrast, Saudi Arabia only abolished slavery in 1962. That same year Yemen abolished slavery and the United Arab Emirates abolished slavery a year later.

The Saudi ruling family did not act out of goodwill. They did so under pressure from President Kennedy. At the time, the House of Saud did not yet control the US economy and foreign policy. The abolition of slavery was a compromise. Kennedy had wanted representative government and civil rights. He had to settle for a belated emancipation.

Slavery has been officially abolished; unofficially it lingers on. There is still a silent unofficial slave trade that is carried on and leading Saudi clerks have insisted that slavery is a part of Islam. Saudis living abroad are often discovered to have domestic workers who live like slaves leading to criminal cases.

The situation is worst in North Africa. Arab colonization largely displaced and suppressed the indigenous peoples, like the Nubians in Egypt. The Lake Nasser project ethnically cleansed the Nubians. Now, like many North African indigenous peoples, they are a persecuted minority in their own land.

Some may argue that, like Islamic terrorism, Islamic slavery is unrelated to Islam. Yet, the Koran and Hadiths justify racial slavery. They discuss Mohammed's trade in black slaves.

Al-Tabari wrote that, "Noah prayed that Ham's descendants' hair would not grow beyond their ears. He also prayed that whenever they met Shem's descendants, they would enslave them." This belief gave a religious reason for the Arab conquests and ethnic cleansing in Africa.

The great Muslim historian Ibn Khaldun justified slavery. He viewed black people as animals. He wrote, "The only people who accept slavery are the Negroes, owing to their low degree of humanity and proximity to the animal stage.""

The legacy of Islam makes the permanent abolition of slavery and racism impossible. In the 19th century, Egypt and its Mamaluk slave empire fell. British attempts to end slavery seemed to have succeeded. But, the new Muslim Brotherhood constitution lifted the old ban on slavery. Mauritania officially outlawed slavery numerous times, but it still widely persists. Saudi Arabia abolished slavery. But, its elite families still have old habits. The Hadiths say Allah chose the Arabs above all others, and the Quraysh above the Arabs. These families, of whom the Hadiths speak, are in the West now.

The oil-rich tyrannies at the heart of the Islamic Gulf are maintained by armies of slave laborers with few rights. The skyscrapers of Dubai and Doha are built with the blood of thousands of foreign workers. They are paid a pittance and can only leave with their masters' approval.

Ali al-Ahmed, a leading Saudi scholar and the director of the Institute for Gulf Affairs, put it bluntly in Foreign Policy magazine. "Blacks, 10% of the population, are banned from judgeships. So are women and Muslims who follow a different version of the faith. The monarchy's religious tradition views blacks as slaves, other Muslims as heretics, and women as half human." There is only one word to describe such a system: Apartheid."

Saudi money funds propaganda that accuses Israel of Apartheid for fighting Saudi-backed terrorists. Meanwhile, the brutal kingdom continues its ancient policy of slavery and repression.

And in North Africa, African migrants look to the West to escape racism in lands colonized by Islam. "Arabs hate black people. And that is not from today, it is in their blood," a young African man named Aboubakr says. "Blacks have no rights here."

To watch a video of Islam's institution of slavery in Sudan today, see below:

Freedom Center pamphlets now available on Kindle: Click here.

Filed Under: Daily Mailer, FrontPage 28

About <u>Daniel Greenfield</u>

Daniel Greenfield, a Shillman Journalism Fellow at the Freedom Center, is a New York writer focusing on radical Islam. He is completing a book on the international challenges America faces in the 21st century.

Mladen Andrijasevic · <u>6 hours ago</u>

I do not think there is a better book on this subject than Bernard Lewis's Race and Slavery in the Middle East: An Historical Enquiry <u>http://www.amazon.com/Race-Slavery-Middle-East-Hi...</u>

Islam authorizes slavery. The Sharia regulates it. Islam has not abolished slavery, and never will, because it is in the Sharia. Islam is predatory.

# Muslims Sexually Enslaving Children: A Global Phenomenon

### By Raymond Ibrahim on September 3, 2014in
### Islam, Muslim Persecution of Christians
### FrontPage Magazine

The Muslim-run sex ring in Rotherham, England, may shock some. It abused 1,400 British children, as young as 11. They were drugged and passed around in cabs and kabob shops. But, this problem is very widespread. In the United Kingdom alone, it's the fifth sex abuse ring led by Muslims to be uncovered.

Some years back in Australia, a group of "Lebanese Muslim youths" raped "Anglo-Celtic teenage girls" in a series of brutal gang attacks." A few years later in the same country, four Muslim Pakistani brothers raped at least 18 Australian women, some as young as 13. In the U.S., a gang of Somalis abducted, bought, sold, raped, and tortured American girls, some as young as 12. Somalia is a Muslim nation that persecutes non-Muslims, mainly Christians.

The question begs itself: If Muslim minorities fear no reprisals in non-Muslim countries, how are Muslims in the Islamic world, where they are dominant, treating their vulnerable non-Muslim minorities?

The answer is a centuries-long, continents-wide account of nonstop sexual predation. Boko Haram's recent abduction and enslavement of nearly 300, mostly Christian, schoolgirls last April in Nigeria is but the tip of the iceberg.

The difference between what happens in Nigeria and what happens in Western nations is based on what I call "Islam's Rule of Numbers." As Muslims increase in number, so do Islamic phenomena. This includes the sexual abuse of "infidel" children and teenagers.

Thus, in the United Kingdom, where Muslims make for a sizeable—and notable—minority, the systematic rape of "subhuman infidels" naturally takes place. But when caught, Muslim minorities, being under "infidel" authority, cry "Islamophobia" and feign innocence.

In Nigeria, however, which is roughly 50 percent Islamic, such "apologetics" are unnecessary. After seizing the nearly 300 schoolgirls, the leader of Boko Haram appeared on videotape boasting that "I abducted your girls. I will sell them on the market, by Allah…. There is a market for selling humans. Allah says I should sell."

It's the same in Pakistan—the nation where many of the United Kingdom's Muslims, including the majority involved in the Rotherham sex ring, come from. See this article for a long list of Christian children—as young as 2-years-old—who were targeted by Muslim men for abduction, enslavement, and rape. In every single case, police do nothing except sometimes side with the Muslim rapists against their "infidel" victims.

Last Easter Sunday, four Muslim men gang-raped a 7-year-old girl, Sara. They left her in "critical condition." Asia News reported, "The police, instead of arresting the culprits, helped a local clan to kidnap the girl's father." This was to 'force the family not to report the story, to reach an agreement with the criminals, and to avoid a religious dispute.'"

In 2010, a woman, Sama, enslaved Kiran George, a Christian girl. She was a dealer of youths sold as prostitutes to wealthy Muslim families. A police officer involved in the sex ring doused Kiran with gasoline, set her on fire, and burned her to death.

A recent report confirms "an estimated 700 cases [of abduction, enslavement, and/or rape in Pakistan] per year involve Christian women,

300 Hindu girls." These are large numbers, given that Christians and Hindus each make up one percent of Pakistan's 97 percent Muslim population.

One can go on and on. In 2011, a Christian group in Egypt exposed a Muslim ring. It was based in the Fatah Mosque in Alexandria. The investigation uncovered a "religious call" plan. It urges young Muslim males in high school and university to approach Coptic girls, aged 9-15, to exploit and blackmail them. The plan aims to sexually compromise Christian girls. It seeks to defile and humiliate them in front of their parents. This would force the girls to flee their homes and use conversion to Islam as a "solution."

In the last three years, about 550 Coptic Christian girls have been abducted and sexually abused by Muslim men. This was especially true under the Muslim Brotherhood, when sexual crimes were rampant.

So, what animates this phenomenon of Muslim on non-Muslim rape? We must call it Muslim rape. Islam is the common factor in these cases. The nations are otherwise diverse, with few things in common except for their large Muslim populations.

On pedophilia, the Koran urges Muslims to emulate Muhammad, Islam's prophet. He was "betrothed" to a six-year-old girl, Aisha, and "consummated" their marriage when she was nine. Islam's clerics often defend child "marriage," even to infants, based on the prophet's example.

As for the subhuman treatment of "infidel" children, this is seen as a right by supremacist Muslims. Discussing the 2010 rape of a 9-year-old Christian girl, local sources in Pakistan put it well: "It is shameful. Such incidents occur frequently. Christian girls are considered goods to be damaged at leisure. Abusing them is a right. According to the [Muslim] community's mentality it is not even a crime. Muslims regard them as spoils of war."

"Spoils of war" is quite correct. The late Majid Khadduri, a top expert on Islamic law, said this about "spoils" in his book, War and Peace in the Law of Islam:

The term spoil (ghanima) is applied specifically to property acquired by force from non-Muslims. It includes, however, not just property, both movable and immovable. It also includes persons, whether asra (prisoners of war) or sabi (women and children). ... If the slave were a woman, the master was permitted to have sexual connection with her as a concubine.

Nor is this limited to academic talk. Last year, Jordanian Sheikh Yasir al-'Ajlawni said Muslims fighting to topple "infidel" President Bashar Assad in Syria may "capture and have sex with" all non-Sunni women, including Shia, Alawites, Christians, Druze, and Yazidis.

Before him, Egyptian Sheikh Ishaq Huwaini lamented how, in Islam's heyday, "You [could] go to the market and buy her [enslaved, infidel concubines for sale] ..." In other words, when I want a sex-slave, I go to the market and pick whichever female I desire and buy her."

To stop sexual immorality among male Muslim youth, Kuwaiti activist Salwa al-Mutairi suggested re-establishing sex slavery, like what was exposed in Rotherham. She said on video that Islam's greatest authorities from Mecca, the city of Islam, all confirmed the legality of sex-slavery to her. According to the Kuwaiti woman:

A Muslim state must first attack a non-Muslim state. Sorry, I mean a Christian state. The women, the future sex-slaves, must be captives of the raid. Is this forbidden? Not at all, according to Islam, sex slaves are not at all forbidden. To the contrary, the rules for sex-slaves differ from those for free women [i.e., Muslim women]. A free woman's body must be covered, except for her face and hands. The sex-slave, however, is kept naked from the bellybutton up. She is different from the free woman. A free woman must be properly married to her husband. But, the sex-slave—he just buys her and that's that. For example, in the Chechnya war, surely there are female Russian captives. So go and buy those and sell them here in Kuwait; better that than have our men engage in forbidden sexual relations. I don't see any problem in this, no problem at all.

What happened in Rotherham is hardly an aberration. Rather, it is Islam coming to town, Muslims growing in numbers. Even Dr. Taj Hargey, a British imam, just confirmed that the majority of the UK's "imams promote grooming rings." He said Muslim men are taught that women are "second-class citizens, little more than possessions." They have absolute authority over them." The imams preach a doctrine that "denigrates all women but treats whites with particular contempt.""

Change "whites" to "non-Muslims." This is not about race, but religion. The 1,400 children in Rotherham share experiences with countless non-Muslim minorities in the Islamic world.

"But, when the forbidden months are past, then fight and slay the pagans wherever ye find them. And, seize them, beleaguer them, and lie in wait for them in every stratagem of war. But, if they repent, and establish regular prayers and practice regular charity, then open the way for them. For, God is Oft-forgiving, Most Merciful." (Sura 9:5).

"Fight those who do not believe in God or the Last Day. Do not accept what God and His Apostle have forbidden. Reject the religion of Truth, even if they are People of the Book (Christians and Jews). Do this until they pay the jizya (tribute) with submission and feel subdued." (Sura 9:29).

There is a battle being waged in Egypt. It is the same battle being fought in various corners of the Islamic world. That battle is part of a war being waged anywhere there is an Islamic educational facility, regardless of age or intellect. The fundamentalists are stuck in the Seventh century and will not advance out of that time frame. One of the leaders in the fight to advance the clock is the current President of Egypt, Egyptian President Sisi.

# Sisi vs. the Islamists: A Battle of Ideas

**by Cynthia Farahat _American Thinker_ March 2, 2022**
*Abridged version of article originally published under the title "Egypt's War of Ideas."*

Andeel, *Mada Masr*, September 9, 2016.

Egypt is in a war of ideas. President Abdel Fattah al-Sisi resists Islamists in a struggle for the future of Egypt and the Middle East. Historic reforms are now taking place in the UAE, Sudan, Bahrain, Morocco, Saudi Arabia, and Egypt. But the path to ideological and religious reform has been most difficult in Egypt.

President Sisi has achieved numerous political, cultural, and economic reforms. In infrastructure and urban development alone, he has implemented 11 thousand projects. Sisi has transformed his government and become Egypt's <u>most moderate president</u>. For the first time in Egypt's history, Sisi appointed a Coptic Christian, Judge Boules Fahmy, to head the Supreme Constitutional Court. Most Egyptian Muslims have backed this precedent. But, a faction of Islamists in the government has resisted reform.

Egypt's largest Islamic institution, al-Azhar University in Cairo, has engaged Sisi in a cold war. Fundamentalists in the university have retaliated against him by targeting intellectuals and reformers who share his vision. For decades, al-Azhar has used Egypt's harsh blasphemy law to start Islamic tribunals in its courts. Since 1981, Egypt has persecuted dissidents for blasphemy. Al-Azhar has targeted them with assassination fatwas.

**Al-Azhar uses Egypt's harsh blasphemy law to target Sisi's allies.**

The main legislative bodies are the constitutional court and parliament. But, al-Azhar is the de facto theocratic body. The constitution's second article says, "the principal source of legislation is Islamic Jurisprudence."" ...

This terror-indoctrinating institution and its madrassas get over 20 billion Egyptian pounds (over $1.2 billion) in annual government funding. For decades, the institution has supported heinous crimes and psychosexual disorders. It has also militarized Islam.

For example, al-Azhar's celebrity sheikh, Abdallah Rushdy, has been a strong advocate for slavery. Rushdy said, «slavery is not a crime. We don›t agree [with seculars] that slavery is a crime nor that it›s bad... why do atheists attempt to force us to agree with them that slavery is a crime? We [al-Azhar scholars] disagree and we believe that there are often advantages to slavery.»

**Abdallah Rushdy**

In 2020, Rushdy also advocated for the fundamentalist sabi theology. It legitimizes the kidnapping, sex trafficking, and rape of non-Muslim women. Rushdy doesn't define sexual intercourse with a sex slave as "rape" when it's perpetrated by an Islamist against a non-Muslim female. He said that the "master and his slave" had a "love affair." It sometimes even ended in "marriage" in Islamic history. Rushdy also advocated for the random sexual assault of women who don›t observe Islamic dress codes.

Al-Azhar even encourages pedophilia by theologically permitting men to marry underage girls. In 2017, al-Azhar scholar Sabri Abdul

Raouf issued a religious edict, mudaga'at al-wada' (farewell coitus). It permits a husband to have sex with his wife one last time after her death. That edict was later condemned by al-Azhar after it created controversy across the Middle East.

**Al-Azhar scholar and professor Sabri Abdul Raouf issued an edict. It authorized necrophilia with one's recently-deceased wife.**

Al-Azhar also legitimized cannibalism, maiming infidels, and torturing "bad Muslims" to death. Some of the most brutal terrorists in history received their jihadist indoctrination at al-Azhar. The author's upcoming book, The Secret Apparatus: The Muslim Brotherhood's Industry of Death, suggests that al-Qaeda was likely founded at al-Azhar University in 1971. It was not, as commonly believed, founded in the mid-1980s in Afghanistan.

President Sisi has been trying to peacefully combat these radical ideas for years. Despite his many historic reforms, Sisi has yet to take firm action against al-Azhar. The university is a security threat. Its hundreds of thousands of students and their Muslim Brotherhood allies are in key government posts. Sisi has delayed a fight with al-Azhar. But, he must cut its funding and remove its leaders' immunity.

**Clockwise from top left: Mohammed Abdallah Nasr, Ahmed Abdu Maher, Islam Behery, and Ibrahim Issa.**

During the past few years, al-Azhar has engaged in a proxy warfare with Sisi by targeting those who adhere to his moderate Islamic philosophy. The victims included Muslim scholars, like Mohammed Abdallah Nasr. They included intellectuals, like attorney Ahmed Abdu Maher. They also included reformers and public figures, like Islam Behery and Ibrahim Issa. Islamists have publicly contacted Abdallah Rushdy for advice on killing Ibrahim Issa and Islam Behery.

A dark event in Western history was the Catholic church's Inquisitions. The church punished heresy to counter dissent. That tyrannical practice has long vanished in the West. But, blasphemy is still punished in Islamic-majority countries.

The result of Egypt's war against radical Islam will have profound implications for the Middle East and the world. The response in the West is critical, yet Sisi has been criticized and Islamists supported. This must change.

**Western leaders need to make a choice between Muslim reformers and jihadist inquisitors.**

An ideological war is underway in the Middle East. Western leaders must choose: join Muslim reformers or the jihadist Muslim Brotherhood. Hiding behind nuanced positions is blatant cowardice.

**Cynthia Farahat is a Fellow at the Middle East Forum and author of *The Secret Apparatus: The Muslim Brotherhood's Industry of Death*.**

# So, who is Allah?

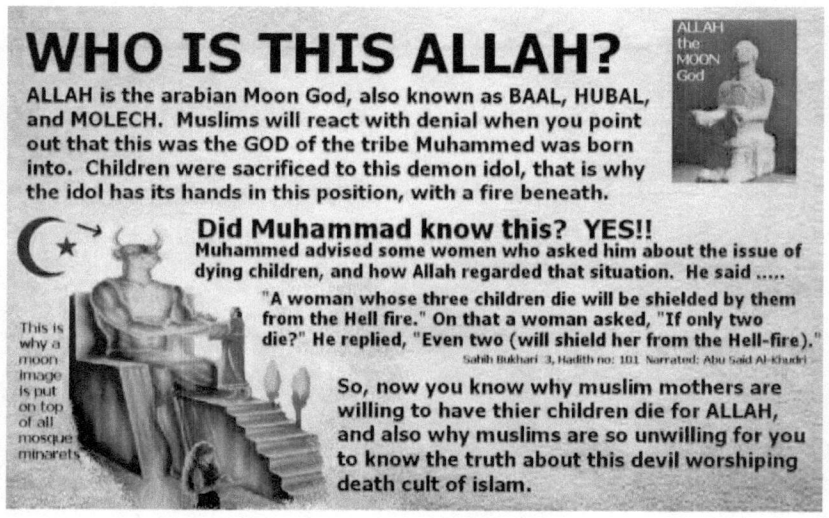

So where did Baal come from? Baal was the central God of Carthage which was destroyed by the Romans. Found under the modern-day city of Tunis is the ruins of the sacked city of Carthage. For a biblical reference, there are several. These are only four I picked, you can find more:

Judges 2:11 And the sons of Israel do the evil thing in the eyes of Jehovah, and serve the **Baal**im,

Judges 2:13 Yea, they forsake Jehovah, and do service to **Baal** and to Ashtaroth.

1 Samuel 12:10: They cried to Jehovah, "We have sinned. We forsook Jehovah and served the Baalim and Ashtaroth. Now, deliver us from our enemies, and we will serve You."

Most importantly

Jeremiah 19.5 I did not command, speak of, or think of it. They built the high places of Baal to burn their sons as burnt offerings to Baal.

What proof do we have of this? In Carthage, we find Tophets. Ancient sources say the Phoenician religion included a ritual of human sacrifice, especially of children. The victims were killed by fire, although it is not clear precisely how. Ancient historians Clitarch and Diodorus said a hearth was set before a bronze statue of the god Baal (or El). The statue had outstretched arms. The victim was placed on them before falling into the fire. They also mention the victims wearing a smiling mask to hide their tears from the god to whom they were being offered. The victim's ashes were then placed in an urn and buried in tombs placed within a dedicated sacred open space surrounded by walls, the tophet.

Tophets are generally located outside the **city** proper and usually to the north. The tophet at **Carthage** has a shrine area with an altar where the sacrifices were made. After the ceremony the ashes of the burnt offering were placed within a vessel. Stones were then placed on top of the funerary urns to seal them and placed within the tophet, sometimes within shaft tombs. From the 6th century BCE, stelae were dedicated to Baal or Tanit and placed on top of the urns instead of stones. Many stelae have an inscription which describes a human blood sacrifice or the substitution of a sheep for a child. The urns were often recycled pots and jars from as far as Corinth and Egypt. They provide a valuable record of Phoenician trade.

This could explain the desire by Rome for the annihilation of Carthage and the thoroughness of with which Rome did wipe Carthage off the map. Child and human sacrifice are especially offensive to Western Philosophies. On the other hand, it is completely acceptable to Islamic beliefs, just look at the number of child suicide bombers.

# Little girl sold for 'organ harvesting'

**By News.com.au October 20, 2013 | 10:16am**

In a first, US warns of dangers of systemic racism in human trafficking report 14 children, toddler among 31 rescued in human trafficking sting Italian police arrest man who provided truck in 2019 UK smuggling deaths

Indian workers held captive and forced to build New Jersey temple, lawsuit claims a young girl has been smuggled out of Africa and sold for organ harvesting, authorities have revealed.

It is the first case of a child trafficked into Britain to provide organs for desperate transplant seekers, reports the Telegraph.

The girl, whose identity has been protected, was taken from Somalia and smuggled into the UK so that her organs could be removed and sold.

A British government report revealed human trafficking has reached record levels, rising by 50 per cent in the last year.

Of the 371 children exploited, most of them were used as slaves or were sexually abused.

They included 95 children from Vietnam, 67 from Nigeria and 25 from China, with other victims coming from Romania and Bangladesh.

The report also said 20 British girls had been victims of human trafficking, in cases where they were raped and exploited by gangs of Asian men.

In 2012, an adult woman was the first reported case of a human brought to the UK by a gang to sell her organs.

The World Health Organization says a shortage of transplant organs has caused a black market for organ trading and "transplant tourism.""

The WHO says payment for organs "is likely to take unfair advantage of the poorest and most vulnerable groups, undermines altruistic donation and leads to profiteering and human trafficking".

Kidneys are the most trafficked organ, because one can be removed with the patient still being able to live a healthy life.

Around 7,000 kidneys are illegally trafficked annually. Illegal organ trading nets more than $1 billion each year.

This story originally appeared on News.com.au.

Filed under human trafficking, Somalia , united kingdom , 10/20/13

Note: There was a movie, "The Island" (2005), starring Scarlett Johansson and Ewan McGregor. It is about people raised as clones to be organ banks for the elite. It is set in a dystopian future. This is worse and is happening now in India, Europe, and elsewhere. Do you have proof it is not happening here in the U.S.? We have over 85,000 missing children, thanks to Secretary Mayorkas. - Glen R. Cook

Part A

# Islamic State Selling Sex Slaves on Facebook

## BREITBART TECH 30 May 2016

It has been revealed that Islamic State sex slaves are being sold on Facebook. Several posts were deleted for advertising young slaves for sale.

"To all the brothers thinking about buying a slave, this one is $8,000," wrote ISIS soldier Abu Assad Almani in a Facebook post. He included a picture of a girl, about 18 years old. "Another sabiyah [slave], also about $8,000... Yay, or nay?" read another one along with a picture of a young girl described to have "weepy red eyes."

Facebook deleted both posts within hours. But, it revealed the depraved lengths ISIS militants will go to in order to fund their jihadi campaign of terror.

Almani's posts were tracked by the Middle East Media Research Institute. They monitor Islamic terrorists online. The Institute saw the posts before Facebook deleted them.

"We have seen much brutality. But, ISIS's content is the most evil we've seen. It has surpassed all else," said Institute director Steven Stalinsky. "Sales of slave girls on social media is just one more example of this."

Comments on the posts were equally as disturbing according to reporter Joby Warrick.

"What makes her worth that price? Does she have an exceptional skill?" wrote one of Almani's friends in a comment one of the photos.

"Nope," replied Almani. "Supply and demand make her that price."

Other comments reportedly mocked the slaves for their looks. They discussed the price of the girls with Almani. They complained that the girls were not wearing a religious veil.

According to the UN's ISIS sex slave price list published last year, children aged between 1 and 9 years old can be sold for around $165. Adolescent girls are mildly cheaper at around $124, while women over 40 who are considered old for ISIS fighters go for as little as $41. Almani's huge price hike shows how much money the Islamic State has lost since last year. Airstrikes destroyed most ISIS-controlled oil rigs and compounds.

Facebook removed the ISIS posts in just a few hours. Some conservative commentators found their posts removed even quicker, and for no good reason. Libertarian Canadian commentator Lauren Southern got a 30-day Facebook ban. This was for defending a popular conservative page admin who had also been banned. The social network even deleted her post. It criticized their politically-biased actions.

Part B

# Facebook Turns Blind Eye to Islamic Slave Trading on its Arabic Platform So As Not to 'Alienate Buyers'

**By Robert Spencer - on September 26, 2021**

If you thought the social media giants couldn't get more evil, think again. Facebook suppresses voices that oppose jihad and Sharia. It ignores Islamic slavery to avoid "alienating" Muslim slave traders.

A September 16 Wall Street Journal article reveals that "a Mexican drug cartel was using Facebook to recruit, train and pay hit men." The behavior was shocking and in clear violation of Facebook's rules. But the company didn't stop the cartel from posting on Facebook or Instagram, the company's photo-sharing site."

Ultimately, Facebook caved under pressure and did the right thing. It took down some offending pages but did little else to shut down the activity until Apple Inc. threatened to remove Facebook's products from the App Store unless it cracked down on the practice. The threat was in response to a BBC story on maids for sale. A Facebook researcher wrote in an internal summary about the episode: "Was this issue known to Facebook before the BBC enquiry and Apple escalation?" The next paragraph begins: "Yes.""

It gets worse. The drug cartel was just one of many evil actors using Facebook with no problem. It banned and blocked conservatives, Trump supporters, and other dissenters of the Left's agenda. An earlier document this year suggested a light touch with Arabic warnings about human trafficking. It was to avoid 'alienating buyers'—Facebook users who buy the contracts of domestic laborers, often in situations akin to slavery."

Slavery is acceptable in Islam. The Qur'an has Allah telling Muhammad that he has given him girls as sex slaves: "Prophet, We have made lawful to you the wives to whom you have granted dowries and the slave girls whom God has given you as booty." (Qur'an 33:50)

Muhammad bought slaves. Jabir (Allah be pleased with him) reported: A slave came and pledged allegiance to Allah's Apostle (may peace be upon him) on migration. The Holy Prophet did not know he was a slave. Then there came his master and demanded him back, whereupon Allah's Apostle (may peace be upon him) said: Sell him to me. And he bought him for two black slaves, and he did not afterwards take allegiance from anyone until he had asked him whether he was a slave (or a free man)." (Muslim 3901)

Muhammad took female Infidel captives as slaves. "Narrated Anas: The Prophet offered the Fajr Prayer near Khaibar when it was still dark and then said, 'Allahu-Akbar! Khaibar is destroyed. For, whenever we approach a hostile nation to fight, then evil will be the morning for those who have been warned.' Then, the Khaibar inhabitants ran on the roads. The Prophet had their warriors killed, their offspring and woman taken as captives. Safiya was amongst the captives. She first came in the share of Dahya Alkali but later on she belonged to the Prophet. The Prophet made her manumission as her 'Mahr.'" (Bukhari 5.59.512) Mahr is bride price: Muhammad freed her and married her. But he didn't do this to all his slaves:

Muhammad owned slaves. "Narrated Anas bin Malik: Allah's Apostle was on a journey. He had a black slave, Anjasha, who was driving the camels very fast. There were women riding on those camels." Allah's Apostle said, 'Waihaka (May Allah be merciful to you), O Anjasha!

Drive slowly (the camels) with the glass vessels (women)!'" (Bukhari 8.73.182) There is no mention of Muhammad's freeing Anjasha.

So, while Facebook cracks down on "Islamophobic" content, it accepts Islamic slavery. After all, one wouldn't want to "alienate" pro-slavery Arabic-speaking Facebook users. Once they come to the United States, -they'll vote Democratic. Conservatives won't. Case closed.

Robert Spencer is the director of Jihad Watch and a Shillman Fellow at the David Horowitz Freedom Center. He is the author of 23 books, many bestsellers. These include The Politically Incorrect Guide to Islam (and the Crusades), The Truth About Muhammad, and The History of Jihad. His latest book is The Critical Qur'an. Follow him on Twitter here. Like him on Facebook here.

# Islam and first-cousin inbreeding make Muslims literally insane

November 25, 2021 John de Nugent English, News 3
**Muslim Inbreeding Has Corrupted Islam's**
**Psyche and the Results Are Alarming**
**30 Sep 2015**
**Islam**
**by Col. Tom Snodgrass**
**http://joemiller.us/2015/09/muslim-inbreeding-has-**
**corrupted-islams-psyche-and-the-results-are-alarming/**

.

**Miller is a very good guy: https://joemiller.us/about/**
*[All photos and captions added by me, John de Nugent]*
**image: http://joemiller.us/wp-content/**
**uploads/29india.xlarge1-150×150.jpg**

Ride Side News had the privilege of e-mailing Nicolai Sennels. He is a Danish psychologist. He has worked on his government's prison psychology programs. They aim to find out why so many juvenile offenders are from the Muslim immigrant community.

His research investigated Muslim inbreeding and its effects on "Islam's psyche." He gained great insight into the "mind of Islam" through thousands of face-to-face talks with disaffected Muslims. Here are his conclusions.**The Interview**

***

**RSN: First Nicolai, would you acquaint the readers with your background, and how you have come by expertise on the Muslim mind. Nicolai** (born 1976): I am a licensed psychologist. My first appearances in the Danish media were about my unorthodox therapy methods. I developed them as the only psychologist at Enderbro, a Copenhagen youth prison (see here and here). I taught the young prisoners about mindfulness meditation. I also developed a special anger management program. I also developed a therapy. It taught criminals with low empathy to take responsibility for their behavior.

In 2008, the prisoners of Enderbro voted the facility as the best prison in Denmark. The leader of Social Services in the Copenhagen municipality concluded that this was due to my work.

At a 2008 conference on immigrant crime, arranged by the Copenhagen municipality, I said to use "criminal Muslims," not "criminal immigrants."" Most criminal immigrants are Muslims.

**Seven out of ten inmates in the Danish youth prisons have immigrant backgrounds,** and almost all of them are Muslims. I was threatened that if I were to discuss my experiences again, I would get fired my job. This story sparked a national debate on free speech. It became a hot topic in the Danish media, even drawing in the Minister of Integration.

I decided to publish a book on my experiences, *"Among Criminal Muslims. "A Psychologist's Experiences from the Copenhagen Municipality" received praise in both the official Psychologists Union's magazine and the newspapers.* I found myself a new job at the Danish Ministry of Defense, and now once again I now work as a psychologist with children and teenagers.

I consulted on the case against Omar Khadr, a convicted terrorist serving in Guantanamo. I also wrote a chapter in the Dutch book Islam: Critical Essays on a Political Religion. It includes work by famous critics of Islam and Muslim immigration. They are Raymond Ibrahim, Hans Jansen, Michael Mannheimer, Ibn Warraq, and Bat Ye'or. Also, I wrote a long list of articles on: the psychology of Islam, its view on women, Muslim culture, and inbreeding in Muslim society.

**RSN: You have written extensively about inbreeding among Muslims. Would you please explain how Islamic culture figures into their criminality.**

**Nicolai: Inbreeding among Muslims are extremely widespread.** About 70 percent of Pakistanis, 45 percent of Arabs, and 25-30 percent of Turks are children of blood-related parents, usually first cousins.

These numbers are staggering. The impacts on Muslims are huge. They affect intelligence, sanity, health, and society. Genetics is, of course, a very touchy subject, especially after Hitler,

But, we must point out a serious problem. It harms millions of children and creates huge issues for their families. They often live in places with no resources for the handicapped.

\*\*\* Some very extreme examples of the results of first-cousin inbreeding in Muslim countries disturbing photos.

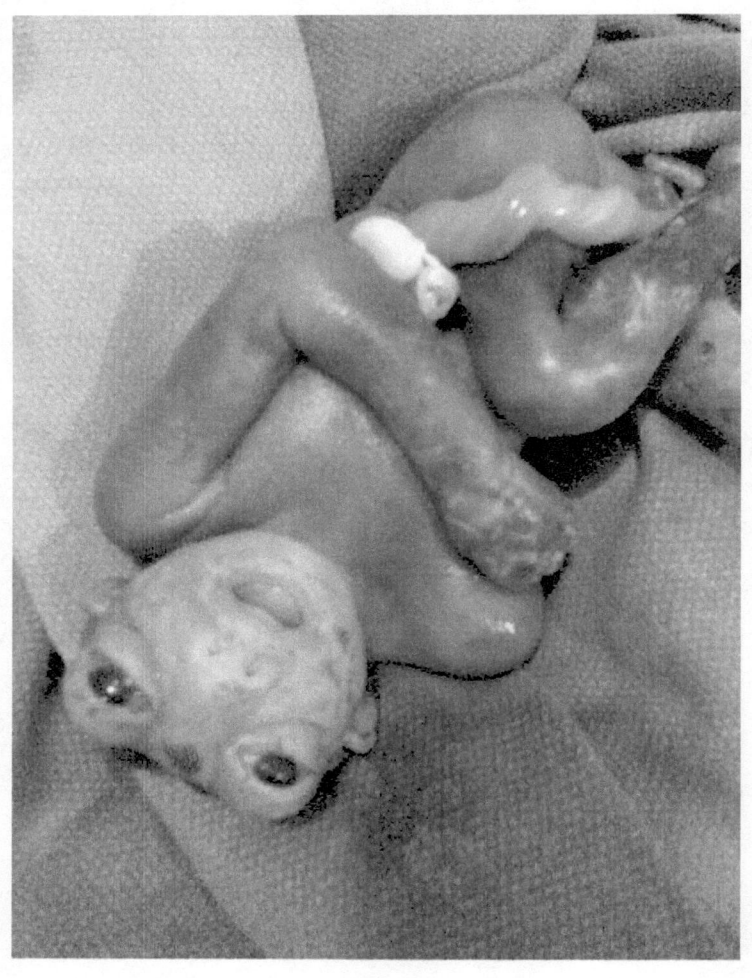

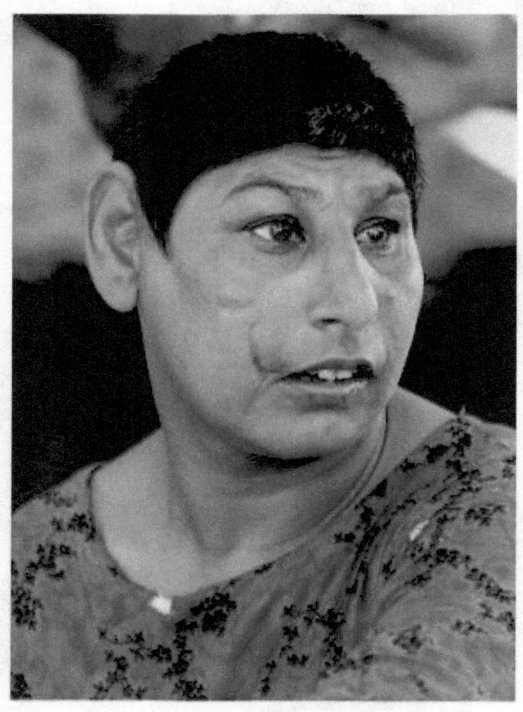

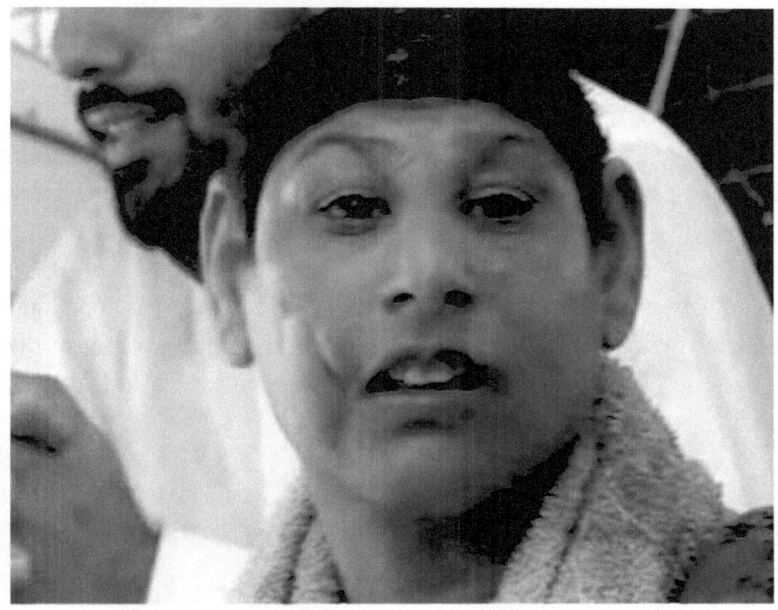

PIC BY IRFAN ALI / CATERS NEWS - (PICTURED: SAIN MUMTAZ) - A young man with a giant head, due to a rare condition, wants to be like his friends. He has become a real-life BFG in his quest for normalcy. Brave Sain Mumtaz, 22, was born with an average size body but an abnormally large head, legs and feet, which have all continued to grow throughout his life. His disorder has left him ill and unable to get around his home on the outskirts of Lahore, Pakistan. As a child, he was told he had Proteus syndrome. It is the same condition as the Elephant Man, Joseph Merrick. It is known for affecting only one side of the body. But the symmetrical deformity of his face and skull suggests he is suffering from a unique variation of the extreme condition. He once thought God had cursed him and that life was pointless. But, thanks to his supportive family and neighbors, Sain has embraced life. Pals call him their giant friend. They are helping keep his spirits high on his quest to find out what is wrong with him and improve his life. SEE CATERS COPY.

***

Taking up the problem of inbreeding in Muslim culture is done out of compassion for the children and the families.

As a psychologist, I am interested in Islam and Muslim culture. I have studied them for over a decade and I have counseled hundreds of Muslims.

And I would say there are several, religious reasons for this very unhealthy practice. One reason is that Muhammad simply allows it. This is done in the Quran's sura 4, which, by the way, also legalizes sex slaves.

Another reason is that consanguineous marriages, as they are called, keep the families' daughters close. This lets them observe if the daughters follow Islamic law, the Sharia.

One third reason is that **Muhammad himself married one of his cousins,**and emulation of Muhammad is a central part of Islamic practice.

**RSN: In your opinion, what role do Muslim genetics play in the Muslim's ability to function in the modern world? Nicolai**: Inbreeding among cousins are connected with long list of risks. These include stillbirths, infant deaths, low IQ, diseases, disabilities, and mental issues.

There also seem to be a clear connection between the negative effects of inbreeding and terrorism. In some cases, people with low intelligence or other mental handicaps have been easy to lure into becoming suicide bombers.

In other cases, martyring oneself can be an honorable end. It may end a life of pain or low status due to handicaps, genetic syndromes, or psychiatric issues.

Also, low intelligence and some psychiatric disorders can result from inbreeding. They are known to increase the risk of delinquent behavior.

Inbreeding, especially over several generations, raises the risk of handicaps and disorders. These can reduce one's ability to function in today's world.

Muslim inbreeding's cognitive effects may explain why non-Western immigrants are over 300% more likely to fail the Danish army's intelligence test than native Danes.

It likely explains, at least in part, why two-thirds of immigrant Arabic schoolchildren are illiterate after 10 years in Danish schools.

The high expenses on **special education** for slow learners consumes **one third of the budget for the Danish schools.**

In three Copenhagen schools for handicapped children, 51% are immigrants. In one school, it's 70%.

These amounts are significantly higher than the share of immigrant children in the municipality, which is 33 percent. One expert said, "The many handicapped children are clear evidence of many intermarried parents in the immigrant families.""

**RSN: It's well-known that Muslims struggle to integrate into Western culture, especially in Europe, or "Eurabia."" What do you think causes this? Nicolai**: Well, to integrate into a culture you have to fulfill three conditions. You have to want it, you have to be able to and you have to be allowed by your family. The more welfare, the less motivation to integrate. You will get food and a place to stay, no matter if you learn the language, earn your own money, and fit in or not.

Due to low education, and possibly inbreeding, many Muslim refugees and migrants cannot. Their cultures differ greatly, often insurmountably, from the West.

Learning the language and getting an education is too hard for them. They can't compete in our high-tech, knowledge-based job market.

Thirdly, many Muslim families do not allow their children to integrate. Western culture values free speech, democracy, and women's equality. These conflict with Islam and Muslim culture in many ways. So, many Muslims see integration as apostasy.

Some young Muslims and Muslim women try to break free of Islam's restrictions. But, the consequences are often so extreme that they deter thousands from trying.

Also, the Quran and the hadiths contain hate speech against non-Muslims and our way of life. This makes it very unnatural to befriend and trust non-Muslims. A recent study by the German state found that 94 percent of Muslims in Germany agreed that immigrants should keep their home country's culture.

The result you see today all over the West, where Muslims tend to group in Muslim areas. Many of these areas are today de facto no-go zones. Here, secular authorities are often threatened and attacked. But, fundamentalist imams, Muslim father groups, and homemade sharia courts are safe to rule.

**RSN: In your experience, what role do Islamic religious authorities play in the life of Muslim immigrant community? What role does the Islamic faith play in the success or failure of Muslim immigrants in integrating into the host culture? Nicolai**: Well, to answer your first question, it is just to look at the statistics. The study from Germany says that 85% of Muslims there are religious or very religious.

A study across Europe found that 75 percent of Muslims there believe the Quran must be taken literally. They think it cannot be interpreted ambiguously.

Many other studies reach similar conclusions. Muslims are more religious than most other groups. They trust their religious books more.

So, religious authorities play an important role in Muslim immigrants' lives.

*Muslim men marry little girls*

It is vital to ensure, [LOL!], that mosques in the West reject, publicly and consistently, the Quran and Hadith verses that tell Muslims to persecute, harm, or kill non-Muslims.

If we do not ensure this, mosques and religious authorities will contribute to the radicalization of Muslims. Unfortunately this has already happened, and now Europe has a deadly serious problem with homegrown jihadis.

80 percent of young Turks in Holland see "nothing wrong" in waging Jihad against non-Muslims. 27% of young French and 14% of young British Muslims under 25 sympathize with the genocidal terror group Islamic State.

This includes most probably the vast majority of young Muslims in these two countries. Take a look at those numbers and then try to imagine what this means to Europe's future. Several of our countries have deployed the military. The police are running out of resources in their desperate efforts to track and contain the threats.

The interesting thing is that Islam is the only religion where, the more people practice and study it, the more violent they become.

[Umm, he is forgetting, or fears discussing, one more semitic religion — Judaism.]

So when it comes to Islam, **more religion means more violence.**

I think many Americans are not aware of what you are letting into your countries for all these months and years.

After decades of Muslim immigration, over half of Europeans oppose it. They reject the spread of Islam in our countries. **I had hoped that the Americans would have learned from our bad example here where I live.** But it seems that your president [Obama] has decided that you should undergo make your own "experiences."

As for your second question about Muslims, look at Europe for the answer.

Islam is opposed to Western, liberal values in so many areas that you can not really call yourself a real Muslim if you also integrate. You might call yourself a "relaxed" or "moderate" Muslim. But, you cannot support free speech, democracy, and the equality of women and non-Muslims. At the same time, you cannot say you follow the Quran and Muhammad's example.

**RSN: In Western circles, Muslim treatment of women is considered oppressive. Do you find that view valid? What role do women play in Islamic culture? I know it varies by country and region. Nicolai**: Islam is obviously suppressive against women. Just read the Quran and the Hadiths. The question is, of course, how much Muslims follow the laws of Allah and his prophet. For sure, there are some variations. Just look at photos of women in Iran before and after the Islamic revolution. It is heart-breaking to see how those beautiful, smiling, free women have become veiled and suppressed in today's Iran.

In some Islamic countries, though it is fewer and fewer, at least non-Muslim women can wear a bikini on the beach.

The role of women in Islamic culture is mainly to signal honor. The honor of the family depends on the women's' willingness to submit themselves to the suppressive laws of Sharia.

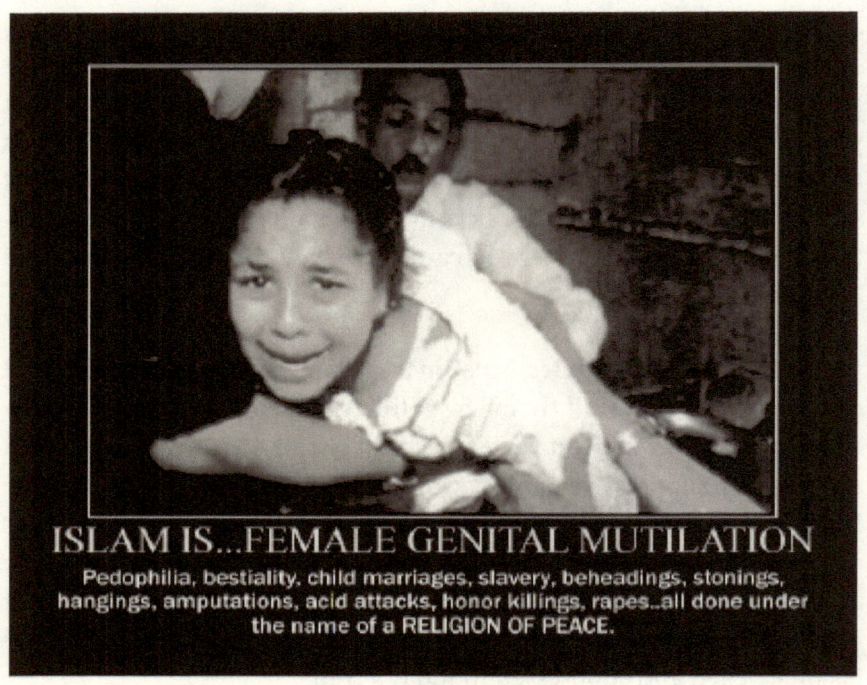

ISLAM IS...FEMALE GENITAL MUTILATION

Pedophilia, bestiality, child marriages, slavery, beheadings, stonings, hangings, amputations, acid attacks, honor killings, rapes..all done under the name of a RELIGION OF PEACE.

As a psychologist, I find it interesting that the religious suppression of Muslim women affects not just the women, but also the men. It simply **changes the men's' sexuality when they are taught that women are impure. Many Muslim men thus develop homosexuality or pedophilia.**

*Hungarian graphic: the EU grows the tree that will hang Europe.*

**Research among Pakistani truck drivers, for instance, shows that 95 percent of them "indulge in sex with ˜boy' helpers."**

Most psychological schools say that homosexuality is not a disorder. It is only if cultural factors cause it. The Afghan culture is the world's most segregated and oppressive to women. It has a practice of using "dancing boys," or basha bareesh. This is a sign of a culture that seems to lead to such behavior.

A US military report from Afghanistan concludes that

*"Homosexual behavior is unusually common among men in the large ethnic group known as Pashtuns. "Pashtun men often have sex with other men. They admire other men and have sexual relationships with boys. They shun women both socially and sexually.""*

The report also described how male Pashtun interpreters spread gonorrhea to each other. When the doctors told them to be more careful, they lied. They said their homosexual activities caused it, but it was from mixing different teas.

A US doctor in Afghanistan had to explain to a local man how to get his wife pregnant. When told what was necessary, the man reacted with disgust. He asked, "How could one desire to be with a woman, whom God has made unclean, when one could be with a man, who is clean?" Surely this must be wrong.'"

RSN: As a psychologist, do you think Muslim views on sexuality promote mental health?

**What are the effects of Muslim sexual practices in regard to their relations with members of the host society? Nicolai:** On the psychological level, one of the most serious consequences of the Islamic view on women is the **extreme lack of romantic love.** The healing power of romantic love requires equality between partners. There must be no fear, no domination, and no one forced.

A lack of love and the freedom to explore each other can cause increased anger and aggression, among other social problems.

One obvious case is the infamous "underwear bomber," Umar Farouk Abdulmutallab. He tried to blow up an airplane in midair on Christmas Day in 2009. Abdulmutallab struggled with sexual fantasies that, according to his Islamic belief, were sinful. In order to mentally combat the sexual fantasies, he tried to fantasize about jihad instead.

In the end he decided to blow up the main cause of his frustrations by hiding the explosives in his underwear, next to his penis.

Islamization of sexuality in our Western countries is already happening. We see this already in the way that non-Muslim men are regularly excluded from public swimming halls. Our secular societies are pressured to build separate baths in sports halls. Our authorities advise women not to wear sexy clothes near refugee centers, etc.

I think our free sexual culture and women's equality in the West contribute to Muslims' alienation here. The Islamic view on marriage, which is often not fully voluntary, accepts rape. **The Quran allows Muslim men to rape non-Muslim women. Combined with the Islamic view on them, this has caused an epidemic of rapes across Western Europe.** Sweden, Holland and UK are hit hardest. Authorities in England estimates that "up to a million" [white] children may have been victims of primarily Pakistani rape gangs. According to one report, **Muslim men are 200 times more prone to rape children than non-Muslim men.** Every rape is a catastrophe to not only the victim but also the victims' family and friends. Life-long traumatization and difficulties in one's sex life are also often a result.

**RSN: Many Western nations are experiencing a large influx of Muslim immigrants. Can we productively integrate so many Muslims into Western societies? This is a concern for both the host society and the immigrants. Nicolai:** Only non-Europeans can ask such a question. Here on our continent it is clear to everybody that it is not possible, and that the consequences are devastating. We must witness, not just economically, our beautiful, historic European towns and cities. Their growing areas are transforming. Our thousand-year-old culture is disappearing and facing hostility.

These areas are often sealed to non-Islamic cultures and values. They now breed jihad-sympathizers on an industrial scale.

It is becoming more and more common that people are talking about the imminent danger of civil war in our cities. Many of us have had to explain to our children why there are armed military and police with automatic rifles on the way to kindergarten and school.

The worst thing is that such conditions are now normal for our kids. They do not know what we have lost. This makes it hard for them to fight to reclaim the safety, freedoms, and culture that nourish the world with European, humanistic values.

**RSN: What advice would you offer the Western world regarding their growing Muslim populations? Nicolai**: Well, I have been working with this topic for so many years. My continent, country, and neighborhood have turned into a dystopian sci-fi movie. I'd have dismissed it if someone had predicted it 20 years ago.

I think we can say for sure now that **integrating Muslims in Western society is not possible.** Of course a few will always want it, be able to, and have their family's consent, but the vast, vast majority will not.

Any society can handle having a few un-integrated individuals. There is enough money to give them money for food and clothing, enough public housing and enough police.

But when there are enough of such individuals to establish a counter-culture in a larger defined area, trouble starts. That is where you can talk about a **critical mass.** And this just takes a few thousand. If you live far away, you may not even notice it. But, if you live close by, you will see your house lose value. Crime rates will rise. There will be less money for welfare. Your children will feel less safe in school.

I think Americans are blind to the risks of inviting tens of thousands of Muslims into your country. You already have problems with gangs and large ghettos. But you have to understand that Muslim ghettos are different from other ghettos. This is because, and this is what Europe learned at such great costs, that Islam is a political religion. It is not just about am a psychologist, nor a politician. I mostly look at the human processes. It is not just about inner states of mind, inner beliefs, inner values. Islam is also about how society must be aligned with Islamic law, the Sharia. And more important is that Islam condones any mean in order to create these changes. These means include violent jihad and jihad through abusing the legal system. It also includes taqiyya, which means lying to advance Islam. And hijrah, which means migrating to conquer non-Islamic land, block by block if necessary.

And more important is that **Islam condones any means** in order to create these changes.

These means include violent jihad and jihad through abusing the legal system. It also includes so-called taqiyya, which means lying to advance Islam. And, hijrah, which means migrating to conquer non-Islamic land, block by block if necessary.

I want you Americans to be aware of this fundamental nature of Islam. **It is not like other religions.** And I hope that you will take a look at Europe and see what is happening here. Our free, safe societies are being suffocated by terror threats and Islamization. We share a basic trust and understanding, as we have the same values.

Europe has many things to offer the world. Our art, our egalitarian values, and our food. But not the naïve approach to Islam and Muslim immigration, which has already cost so much on so many levels. There is a very interesting documentary called "Muslims in Europe", which might be good to spread in the USA.

### End of Interview Conclusion

I recommend an RSN article, "Muslim Pedophiles, Feminists And Future Civil War." It is about Europe's decline due to Islam. It has an excellent documentary on the topic." It offers a disturbing view of Islamic depravity in Great Britain.

Sennels' findings, and the linked doc and article, are clear. Islam is contaminating Europe's culture. It cannot peacefully coexist with Western civilization in the same space.

Muslim inbreeding has corrupted Islam's psyche. Together with jihad, it makes Islam incompatible with a civilization based on Enlightenment principles.

(For more from the author of "Muslim Inbreeding Has Corrupted Islam's Psyche and the Results Are Alarming")
Read    more:    **http://joemiller.us/2015/09/muslim-inbreeding-has-corrupted-islams-psyche-and-the-results-are-alarming/#ixzz449wkDjI3**
You might also like
**Did Weiner Secretly Convert to Islam to Marry a Muslim?**
**Video: Congressman says US schools should adopt Koran, model Islamic Madrassas**
**Sudan President: non-Muslims will have no rights under sharia constitution**
**Obama circumvents Congress again, giving $1.5 billion to Muslim Brotherhood**
**Muslim nations' fertility rates "have taken a steeper dive than any countries in history"**
**Video: Hamas Founder's son claims Islam is "a religion of war," Muhammad author of extremism, terror**

**Intell Sources 20July 2024**
Topics
News

| 1. | *Newsletter * | | https://www.gatestoneinstitute.org/ |
|----|---------------|---------------|-------------------------------------|
| 2. | *News* | Robert Spencer | https://www.jihadwatch.org/ |
| 3. | *News* | Pamela Gellar | https://gellerreport.com/ |
| 4. | *News Video* | | https://www.memri.org/tv |

5. **\*News\***        **https://www.counterextremism.com**

6. *\*News China\**    **https://www.scmp.com/news**    *South China Sea*

7. **\*News China\***    **https://experts.scmp.com/latest-news**

8. **\*News**    https://www.analyzingamerica.org/

9. \*News    http://www.imgclients.com/ic/site/hotspots

10. \*News    https://www.investigativeproject.org/

11. News \$\$\$    https://www.trackingterrorism.org/

12. News    https://www.intelcenter.com/

13. **\*News**    **https://www.meforum.org/**

14. **\*News**    **https://www.africaintelligence.com/**

15. News \$\$\$    https://thefederalist.com/

16. Left News    https://theintercept.com

17. \*News\*    https://www.politico.com/

18. News    https://www.govexec.com    Government Executive

## Authors

1. Author/    Bridget Gabriel    https://www.actforamerica.org/

2. Author/ FGM    Ayaan Ali Hirsi    https://www.theahafoundation.org/

3. Author    Wafa Sultan    http://wafasultan.blogspot.com

4. **Author**    **Raymond Ibrahim**    **http://www.raymondibrahim.com/**

5. Author    Daniel Pipes    http://www.danielpipes.org/

## Research

6. **Research**    **https://www.hudson.org/**

7. \*News    http://www.imgclients.com/ic/site/hotspots

8. \*News    Most Wanted Fugitives - Florida Department of Highway Safety and Motor Vehicles (flhsmv.gov)

9. \*News\*    http://www.targetofopportunity.com/palestinian_truth.htm

10. News \$\$\$    https://www.stratfor.com/    Subscriber

11. Leftwing research    https://www.globalresearch.ca/

12. Research    https://brownstone.org/articles

13. Research    https://www.brookings.edu/    Brookings Institute

14. **Energy News**    **https://www.energyintel.com/**    **EVs vs Petrol**

15. Think Tank    https://www.csis.org/    Center for Strategic and International Studies

## Countries

16. **News**    **Japan**      **http://the-japan-news.com/news/business**
17. **News**    **Arab**      **http://www.arabnews.com/**
18. **News**    **Iran**      **http://en.farsnews.com/**
19. **News**    **Germany**      **https://www.dw.com/en**
20. **News**    **Denmark**      **https://www.thelocal.dk**
21. **News**      **https://www.indiandefensenews.in**    *India Defense*
22. *News*      **https://defence.pk**      *Pakistan Defense*
23. ***News   Australia***    **https://www.skynews.com.au/**
24. News Israel/World    https://jcpa.org/
25. Argentina    https://www.batimes.com.ar
26. Israel    https://www.jns.org/
27. Canada    https://www.youtube.com/@theplebreporter/featured
28. Egypt    https://english.aham.org.eg
29. India    https://www.theweek.in/
30. **Turkey**    **https://turkeypurge.com/**
31. Japan/Asia    https://asia.nikkei.com/
32. **Turkey**    **https://www.aa.com.tr/en**
33. **Russia**    **https://www.themoscowtimes.com/**
34. Russia    https://www.rbth.com/history/
35. North Korea    https://pscore.org/home/      Defectors
36. India (Hindi)    https://www.indiatoday.in/world/      **Learn**
37. **Middle East**    **https://www.middleeastmonitor.com**
38. **South America**    **https://www.world-newspapers.com/countries/ south-america**
39. Cities    https://www.city-journal.org/

## Medical

40. *Medical    https://www.medpagetoday.com
41. Medical    https://www.medicinenet.com
42. **\*Medical**    **https://www.ehstoday.com/**   **emergency health systems**
43. Health    https://www.healthline.com/
44. NIH      https://nihrecord.nih.gov/past-issues
45. **\*Medical**    **https://interestingengineering.com**      **Medical/ anything else computer car etc.**    **CUTTING EDGE**

## Science

46. SCIENCE    https://cosmosmagazine.com    from    Australia science
47. **\*Earthquake https://earthquake.usgs.gov/earthquakes/map**    **Volcanos**
48. **\*Tropical Storms**    **https://www.tropicaltidbits.com**

49. Tropical Storms    https://www.wunderground.com/hurricane
50. **Tropical Storms    https://www.nhc.noaa.gov**
51. Weather Local    https://www.weather.gov
52. **Solar Storms    https://spaceweather.com/**
53. Genetics    https://geneticliteracyproject.org/
54. Darwin    https://www.discovery.org/    Store-AI, Darwin,
    ETC
55. Geoengineering    https://zerogeoengineering.com/

## Economics
56. **\*Finance\*    https://mises.org/wire**
57. Economics    https://fee.org/    Foundation for Economic Education
58. Academic journal library    https://www.jstor.org/    Economics

## MILITARY
59. **Maritime News    https://gcaptain.com**
60. Military News:    Navy    Times= https://www.navytimes.com/
    • https://www.armytimes.com/    https://www.airforcetimes.com/
    • https://www.marinecorpstimes.com    https://www.militarytimes.com/
61. **Intell Lasers    MisterrRobots.com    Maui Fires**
62. **Intell Lasers    Stevevavis.com    Maui Fires**
63. **Biowarfare    https://www.ncbi.nlm.nih.gov/pmc/articles/PMC1326439/
    Israel**
64. **Biowarfare    https://www.dw.com/en/
    covid-vaccines-as-passive-biological-warfare-in-middle-east/a-56471435**
65. NATO    https://www.nato.int/cps/en/natohq/news.htm
66. Intell    http://www.sofx.com    Special Operations Forces
                                        Newsletter
67. **Survival Planning    https://tipsforsurvivalists.com**

## United States Preparation
68. **News    https://americascivilwarrising.org/**
69. Politics vs reality    https://wentworthreport.com
70. Persecution    https://www.intoleranceagainstchristians.eu
71. Persecution    https://eclj.org/religious-freedom/un/
    the-label-christianophobia-in-human-rights-law

**\*-used regularly    \$-subscribe versus free**

# US approved thousands of child bride requests over past decade

**Associated Press**

WASHINGTON – The AP obtained government data. It shows that, over the past decade, thousands of requests by men to bring in child and adolescent brides to the U.S. were approved. In one case, a 49-year-old man applied for admission for a 15-year-old girl.

The approvals are legal: The Immigration and Nationality Act does not set minimum age requirements. In weighing petitions for spouses or fiancées, U.S. Citizenship and Immigration Services checks if the marriage is legal in the home country. Then, it checks if the marriage is legal in the petitioner's state.

But, the data raises questions about the immigration system. It may be enabling forced marriage. U.S. laws may be making the problem worse, despite efforts to limit child and forced marriage. In the U.S., adult-minor marriages are not uncommon. Most states allow children to marry, but with some restrictions.

A 2017 Senate report showed over 5,000 cases of adults petitioning for minors. It also found nearly 3,000 cases of minors seeking to bring in older spouses or fiancés.

Some victims of forced marriage say the lure of a U.S. passport combined with lax U.S. marriage laws are partly fueling the petitions.

In this Feb. 2, 2016, file photo, Naila Amin, 26, looks out from a classroom window at Nassau Community College in Garden City, N.Y.

"My passport ruined my life," said Naila Amin, a dual citizen from Pakistan who grew up in New York City.

She was forcibly married at 13 in Pakistan and applied for papers for her 26-year-old husband to come to the country.

"People die to come to America," she said. "I was a passport to him. They all wanted him here, and that was the way to do it."

Amin, now 29, said she was betrothed to her first cousin Tariq when she was just 8 and he was 21. The petition was eventually terminated after she ran away. She said the ordeal cost her a childhood. She was in and out of foster care and group homes, and it took a while to get her life on track.

"I was a child. I want to know: Why weren't any red flags raised? Whoever was processing this application, they don't look at it? They don't think?" Amin asked.

There is a two-step process for obtaining U.S. immigration visas and green cards. Petitions are first considered by USCIS. If granted, they must be approved by the State Department. Overall, there were 3.5 million petitions received from budget years 2007 through 2017.

Over that period, there were 5,556 approvals for those seeking to bring minor spouses or fiancees, and 2,926 approvals by minors seeking to bring in older spouses, according to the data. Additionally, there were 204 for minors by minors. Petitions can be filed by U.S. citizens or permanent residents.

"It indicates a problem. "It shows a loophole we must close," Republican Sen. Ron Johnson, chair of the Senate Homeland Security Committee, told the AP.

In nearly all the cases, the girls were the younger person in the relationship. In 149 instances, the adult was older than 40, and in 28 cases the adult was over 50, the committee found. Among the examples: In 2011, immigration officials approved a 14-year-old's petition for a 48-year-old spouse in Jamaica. A petition from a 71-year-old man was approved in 2013 for his 17-year-old wife in Guatemala.

There are no nationwide statistics on child marriage, but data from a few states suggests it is far from rare. State laws generally set 18 as the minimum age for marriage, yet every state allows exceptions. Most states let 16- and 17-year-olds marry with parental consent. Some states, like New York, Virginia, and Maryland, allow children under 16 to marry with court permission.

Fraidy Reiss, head of Unchained at Last, campaigns against coerced marriage. She researched data from her home state of New Jersey. She determined that nearly 4,000 minors, mostly girls, were married in the state from 1995 to 2012, including 178 who were under 15.

"This is a problem both domestically and in terms of immigration," she said.

Reiss, 19 when her Orthodox Jewish family forced her into an abusive marriage, said that often, cases of child marriage via parental consent involve coercion. A girl is often forced to marry against her will.

"They are subjected to a lifetime of domestic servitude and rape," she said. "And the government is not only complicit; they're stamping this and saying: Go ahead."

The data was requested in 2017 by Johnson and then-Missouri Sen. Claire McCaskill, the committee's top Democrat. Johnson said it took a year to get the information, showing there needs to be a better system to track and vet the petitions.

"Our immigration system may unintentionally shield the abuse of women and children," the senators said in the letter.

USCIS didn't know how many approvals the State Department granted. But, only about 2.6 percent of spousal or fiancée claims are rejected.

Separately, the data show some 4,749 minor spouses or fiancees received green cards to live in the U.S. over that same 10-year period.

L. Francis Cissna, head of USCIS, wrote to the committee. Their request sparked discussion within the agency on preventing forced minor marriages. The agency noticed some issues in how the data was collected and has resolved them. Officials also created a flagging system. It requires verification of the birthdate whenever a minor is detected.

The country where most requests came from was Mexico, followed by Pakistan, Jordan, the Dominican Republic and Yemen. Middle Eastern nationals had the highest percentage of overall approved petitions.

(Note: If Islam reaches 10% of a nation's population, it will become Islamic. Only drastic measures can prevent this due to the Baby Jihad.) - Glen R. Cook, 6)

Are you ready for this to happen in the United States say in Michigan among say the Somali refugees or in New York among the illegal immigrants?

### Rotherham child abuse scandal

Prof Alexis Jay found that 1,400 children were sexually abused in Rotherham between 1997 and 2013.

**A new report says police in Rotherham were not equipped to deal with widespread child sex abuse that plagued the town for over 15 years. The long-awaited findings from the police watchdog are the**

latest in a series of inquiries into a scandal that has cast a shadow over South Yorkshire.

Operation Linden was a series of investigations by the IOPC. They looked at South Yorkshire Police's response to child sexual abuse claims in Rotherham from 1997 to 2013.

The watchdog has found that systemic problems meant **the force failed to recognise the scale of the problem**.

It echoes Prof Alexis Jay's 2014 report that found 1,400 children in the town were targeted by grooming gangs during the period.

BBC News looks at what prompted her report and what happened after its publication.

**What happened in Rotherham?**

In September 2012, The Times published an article. It revealed that a 2010 police report warned of thousands of child sexual exploitation crimes. They were being committed each year in South Yorkshire by networks of Asian men.

The paper said that, for decades, police and child protection agencies in Rotherham knew of these crimes. Yet, they went unprosecuted.

Rotherham Borough Council, South Yorkshire Police, and other agencies set up a team to investigate child sexual exploitation (CSE) after an article raised concerns.

The council would go on to commission an independent inquiry to be led by Prof Alexis Jay.

Her 2014 report found at least 1,400 children were sexually abused. It detailed how men, mostly of Pakistani heritage, raped, trafficked, abducted, beat, and intimidated girls as young as 11.

Council leader Roger Stone resigned immediately after its publication. In the next six months, the CEO, Martin Kimber, and the children's services directors, Joyce Thacker and her predecessor, resigned. So did the Police and Crime Commissioner, Shaun Wright. Wright had previously headed the department from 2005 to 2010.

It also led to the council being taken over by **government-appointed commissioners in 2015** after a report found it was «not fit for purpose».

**What is Operation Linden?**

In 2014, the IOPC launched Operation Linden. It aimed to examine how South Yorkshire Police responded to child sexual abuse complaints after the Jay Report was published.

It undertook 91 investigations from 2014 to 2018. They covered 265 allegations by 51 complainants. Its final investigation took place in 2020.

Of those complainants 44 were survivors of abuse and exploitation.

The IOPC investigated 47 officers. Eight had a case to answer for misconduct. Six had a case to answer for gross misconduct.

In many cases, the officer had retired and, due to legislation in place at the time, could not face disciplinary action.

However, five of these officers received sanctions ranging from management action up to a final written warning.

A sixth faced a misconduct hearing arranged by the force earlier this year and the case was found not proven by the independent panel.

Of the 164 allegations the IOPC looked into where an officer's conduct was not under investigation, it upheld 43 complaints.

IOPC Director of Major Investigations Steve Noonan said it was "an extremely complex piece of work - the second biggest operation we have ever carried out.""

It has also made 13 recommendations to South Yorkshire Police and the College of Policing. This was in addition to examining officers' conduct.

Among those are a recommendation to use abuse survivors' voices in training for officers dealing with child sexual abuse. Also, to review the law on offences committed by groomed and exploited young people.

**What is Operation Stovewood?**

After the Jay Report, the Chief Constable of South Yorkshire Police asked the National Crime Agency (NCA) to lead an independent investigation into abuse allegations in Rotherham from 1997 to 2013.

Called Operation Stovewood, it is the UK's largest probe into non-familial child sexual exploitation and abuse.

About 40 investigations are underway, with 200 officers, mostly from South Yorkshire, working on them.

The NCA said 20 people have been convicted so far due to the operation. There have been over 150 arrests, and it expects those numbers to rise.

Courtesy of BBC News

# The Rape and The Mutilation

Recently the New York Post reported a Moslem man raped his twenty four year old wife and the performed the Hafuud on her. The Post did not ask any of the critical questions like why did he do this and what is result of his actions.

http://www.barenakedislam.com/2014/10/08/muslim-man-in-manhattan-performs-female-genital-mutilation-on-his-young-wife-after-anally-raping-her/

NY Post (h/t next instinct) Moussa Diarra, 48, wanted anal sex with a 24-year-old. When she said no, he raped her, police said. He sodomized her before performing the horrific circumcision around 9 p.m. Sept. 14, the woman told cops.

The victim reported the assault about a week later, police said. Diarra, from Africa, was arrested Sept. 23, court records show. Female genital mutilation is still common there. He was indicted by a grand jury six days later. He is charged with a forcible sex act, aggravated sex abuse by compulsion, attempted assault with intent to disfigure or dismember and assault with intent to cause physical injury with a weapon, court records show.

He is being held at the Manhattan Detention Center in lieu of $20,000 cash bail or $40,000 bond. He is scheduled to appear in court Oct. 27.

The Koran states that women are to be circumcised. No one questions what this means to Moslem women and men.

First, what is the hafuud? The hafuud is the barbaric Moslem practice of removing the external female genitalia: the labia, major and minor, and the clitoris. This is done without anesthesia. So, every painful cut is fully felt. It removes any hope of being a female sexual being. This means the victim has to be held down to restrain her from getting away from the butcher who is mutilating her. There is no age limit. This means girls from birth till marriage and beyond are subject to the knife. If a woman converts, her husband or any male protector can order her to be mutilated to protect her honor regardless of her feelings. By the way, the choice of implement for the cutting can be any of the following: sharp stone, razor, glass, knife, or any other sharp implement. It may be reuse without cleaning on as many as thirty girls in one shot.

Second, the results of the cutting leaves the women permanently disable as a sexual being. Instead of being a vibrant feeling partner, she becomes a baby factory and a set of holes. As a result a Moslem male is never ever able to find or have a fully engaged Moslem sexual partner. To find a fully responsive sexual partner, he must find a woman of another religion. She could be Jewish, Christian, Hindu, or Buddhist. She just can't be Muslim. This leads to Moslem rape gangs and similar problems throughout the world.

# A Secret Network

Michigan: A Muslim doctor is charged with female genital mutilation. She is part of a 'secret network' performing the procedure in the US.

SEP 18, 2021 5:00 PM BY ROBERT SPENCER

We hear the opposite from Western propagandists. But, FGM is justified in Islamic law. Some non-Muslims practice it, but only in majority-Muslim areas where Islamic culture, mores, and law dominate.

"It is a religious thing. Do you want to change religion?" said one Egyptian in response to a campaign to eradicate female genital mutilation. "You only listen to what the West is saying."

The media ignores that FGM is mandated in Islamic law: "Circumcision is obligatory (for every male and female) (by cutting off the piece of skin on the glans of the penis of the male, but circumcision of the female is by cutting out the bazr 'clitoris' [this is called khufaadh 'female circumcision'])."" — Umdat al-Salik e4.3, translated by Mark Durie, The Third Choice, p. 64

Why is it obligatory? It is believed that Muhammad said: "Abu al-Malih ibn Usama's father relates that the Prophet said: 'Circumcision is a law for men and a preservation of honour for women.'" — Ahmad Ibn Hanbal 5:75

"Narrated Umm Atiyyah al-Ansariyyah: A woman used to perform circumcision in Medina. The Prophet (peace be upon him) said to her:

'Do not cut severely as that is better for a woman and more desirable for a husband.'" — Abu Dawud 41:5251

That hadith is weak. But, this one is sahih (reliable): "Aishah narrated: 'When the circumcised meet, then Ghusl is required.' Myself and Allah's Messenger did that, so we performed Ghusl.'" — Jami` at-Tirmidhi 108

If Muhammad had the genitals of his favorite wife, Aisha, mutilated, that is a strong endorsement of the practice. He is an "excellent example" (Qur'an 33:21) for Muslims.

Why does it matter whether or not FGM is Islamic? Because the practice will never be eradicated if its root causes are not confronted. For some, a belief that Allah and Muhammad want it done will override all else, in the U.S. and everywhere.

"Muslim ER doctor charged with female genital mutilation of nine girls aged just seven 'was part of secret network which traveled across US to perform agonizing procedure,' Detroit court hears," by Brian Stieglitz, DailyMail.com, September 16, 2021 (thanks to Henry):

A Muslim doctor on trial for genital mutilation of nine seven-year-old girls was part of a secret network of physicians. Federal prosecutors say they traveled across the country to perform the brutal procedure.

In November 2018, Dr. Jumana Nagarwala was cleared of charges of female genital mutilation. A federal judge ruled that a law banning the practice was unconstitutional. This was the nation's first case of its kind.

But the Michigan doctor faces an obstruction charge for allegedly hiding information during the trial. He was back in court Thursday. That saw prosecutors reveal that doctors in California and Illinois were also cutting young girls as part of a religious rite in the esoteric Indian Muslim sect, Dawoodi Bohras, according to the Detroit Free Press.

Nagarwala was charged with mutilation, conspiracy, and obstruction. This was along with Dr. Fakhruddin Attar, who allowed her to perform surgeries at his Detroit-area clinic.

The same charges were brought against Attar's wife, Farida, and a woman named Tahera Shafiq, who helped in the procedure. Four women tricked their daughters into going to the suburban clinic for religious reasons.

In November 2018, US District Judge Bernard Friedman dismissed all but one obstruction charge against Nagarwala, Attar, his wife Farida, and Shafiq. He declared a 1996 federal law banning the practice unconstitutional. It's up to the states to regulate female genital mutilation.

The obstruction trial was underway until the coronavirus pandemic hit and brought it to a halt. In March, prosecutors issued a new indictment with five charges. They included conspiracy to make false statements and witness tampering, the Detroit Free Press reported.

Prosecutors argue that Nagarwala and her three cohorts lied to the FBI about their mutilations. They also intimidated others to lie if the FBI asked about it.

The four defendants requested Thursday's hearing to dismiss the case. They argued that the prosecutors were pursuing the new charges out of retaliation.

The defense argued in court filings, seen by the Detroit Free Press, that 'the government is acting with extreme prosecutorial vindictiveness in issuing yet another superseding indictment nearly half a decade after charges were first issued.' They added that the new charges are 'retaliation for the defense successfully decimating the government's case.'

Friedman said Thursday he would consider their arguments. But, he was still reviewing the new indictment and would decide later.

Nagarwala, an ER doctor at Henry Ford Health System, was arrested in April 2017. Two young girls accused her of mutilating them earlier that year.

She denied the allegations. She was performing a religious practice for families in the Dawoodi Bohra Muslim sect. It only involved scraping the girls' genitalia, as per the custom.

But doctors' reports obtained by the Detroit Free Press show the children suffered more severe injuries. These included scarring, a small tear, and lacerations. There also appeared to be a surgical removal of a portion of their genitalia.

# Muslim Doctors - Use At Your Own Risk

## Muslim Doctors

As a matter of your own survival, when ever you have to deal with a Doctor for a Medical Emergency, ALWAYS ask if the Doctor is Muslim. If you find out the Doctor is, FIND ANOTHER DOCTOR. I destroyed my rotator cuff. I got taken to the ER in Broward General in Fort Lauderdale, Florida. The Doctor was female Muslim Doctor. The Doctor came in talked with me and left. She came back a while later with a prescription for pain pills and a list of Orthopedic specialists. The female Doctor did not touch me any way. There was no X-rays, no MRIs, no Ultrasounds, nothing. I sked her if she was going to examine the joint. She said rather emphatically no. I asked why, She said she was Muslim and she was not allowed to. I asked how she knew what to do. Her reply scared me, "I just read the notes when you got here." We did not do any real discussion about limitations or what the damage was when I got there, I told them I fell.

Now Muslim Doctors are may or may not be trustworthy and the rule of you can never tell when one will become a Jihadi applies. The following is just a short overview of the size of the problem.

Part A

Lara Kollab

<u>Heavy.com</u> - <u>News</u> -<u>Breaking News</u>

Lara Kollab: 5 Fast Facts You Need to Know By Tom Cleary Updated Jan 4, 2019 at 6:19pm

Twitter Lara Kollab.

A former Cleveland Clinic resident has sparked global outrage. This followed the discovery of her anti-Semitic social media posts. Lara Kollab, a 27-year-old recent medical school graduate, posted several offensive tweets on a personal Twitter account she used for many years. The tweets were discovered by the Canary Mission, a blacklist website that posts information on pro-Palestine students and professors.

"Lara Kollab has called for violence against Jews," the Canary Mission wrote. "She spread anti-Semitism, trivialized the Holocaust, defended Hamas, and supported terrorists on Twitter." The Canary Mission is controversial. But, Heavy and other outlets confirmed its information. The tweets were posted while Kollab was in college and medical school.

Kollab was using the Twitter handle @ellekay_, an apparent reference to her initials. She had the name Lara on her profile and a Facebook page connected to her also used the name Elle Kay. Kollab's anonymous Twitter account gave biographical details. They match confirmed info, including the medical school she attended. Kollab also tweeted about a service trip to Honduras on the @ellekay_ account that Heavy confirmed Kollab took part in. Kollab also revealed her identity on Twitter. In April 2012, she tweeted a friend, "can you do me a favor and search 'lara kollab' and see if my profile comes up still :).""

Kollab has deleted her social media, including her anti-Semitic tweets. She has not commented on the tweets or the interest in them.

On January 4, Kollab issued an apology through a law firm.

"Old comments on my Twitter account have resurfaced. They caused pain and a public outcry." "I sincerely and unequivocally apologize for the hurtful language in those posts," Kollab said in a statement sent to Heavy on January 4.

Ziad Tayeh, of the Cleveland-based Tayeh Law Offices. "This statement does not excuse the posts. But, it shows those words do not reflect who I am and my principles today.""

You can read her full apology below:

Old comments on my Twitter account have surfaced. They are causing pain, anguish, and a public outcry. I wish sincerely and unequivocally to apologize for the offensive and hurtful language contained in those posts. This statement does not excuse the posts. It shows those words do not reflect who I am and my principles today.

I visited Israel and the Palestinian Territories every summer throughout my adolescent years. I became incensed at the suffering of the Palestinians under the Israeli occupation. The occupation's injustice and brutality worry me. Every human rights champion must work for a just, peaceful end to this crisis.

As a girl in my teens and early twenties, I struggled to express my intense feelings about what I saw in my ancestral land. Like many young people, I lacked life experience. So, I made insensitive remarks and thoughtless, passionate statements. I didn't realize they would hurt and offend people.

These posts were made years before I was accepted into medical school, when I was a naïve, and impressionable girl barely out of high school. I matured into a young adult in college and medical school. I adopted strong values of inclusion, tolerance, and humanity. I take my profession and the Hippocratic Oath seriously. I would never harm a patient seeking medical care. As a physician, I will always strive to give the best medical treatment to all people, regardless of their race, religion, ethnicity, or culture.

I have learned from this experience and am sorry for the pain I have caused. I pray that the Jewish community will understand and forgive me. I hope to make amends so that we can move forward and work together towards a better future for us all.

Here's what you need to know about Dr. Lara Kollab:

------------------------------------------------

1. Kollab's Tweets, Which Were Posted Between 2011 & 2017, Include Statements Calling Jews 'Dogs,' Comparing Israel to Nazi Germany & Diminishing the Holocaust Because 'the (People) Who Were in it Now Kill My (People)'

A tweet by Lara Kollab.

While Lara Kollab has deleted her Twitter account, many of her tweets were preserved by the Canary Mission. "She has also compared Israel to Nazi Germany, spread anti-Semitic conspiracy theories and hatred of Israel, and accused Israel of exploiting the Holocaust," the Canary Mission said on its website. "Kollab is a supporter of the Boycott, Divestment, Sanctions (BDS) movement and a supporter of Students for Justice in Palestine (SJP). She is also is affiliated with Al Awda."

In a tweet, Kollab, a college student, told a friend she would give the wrong medication to Jewish patients when she became a doctor. She wrote in the January 2, 2012, tweet, "hahha ewww.. ill purposely give all the yahood [Jews] the wrong meds…"

On December 8, 2012, Kollab tweeted, "After failed diplomacy, our aim is to defeat the Zionist state through force," in reply to a tweet that "peace won't come by killing every Zionist." There has to be diplomacy."

Kollab tweeted on August 27, 2013, "look, Haifa is sweet (nice), but it's full of Jewish dogs, and it looks like America, meaning, it wasn't that special to me." Kollab also directed her antisemitism at people who lived in the city where she was attending school. She tweeted on April 23, 2013, "Annoying to go to school in a city full of Jews because everywhere I go I hear about the wonderful israel. About to tell this guy to stfu."

She also tweeted about the Holocaust. On October 22, 2012, she wrote, "After this debate, I have to watch a movie on the holocaust and write a paper on it. I am going to be brutally unsympathetic. #sorrynotsorry." On October 11, 2012, she tweeted, "If I have to write a paper about the holocaust, I'm going to bring palestine into it and my professor better like it." When someone replied saying that the Holocaust never happened, Kollab responded, " I think it did happen, it's just exaggerated and the victimization of the jews (ignoring the others killed) is overdone."

Kollab tweeted on October 9, 2012, "Of course the only prejudice my class focuses on is US racism against African Americans and the Holocaust. Poor Jews. They're so oppressed." On that same day, she also tweeted, "I don't mean to sound insensitive but I have a REALLY hard time feeling bad about Holocaust seeing as the ppl who were in it now kill my ppl," and "So hard for me to not roll my eyes when the prof was saying that for our midterm, we have to watch a movie about the Holocaust+write a paper."

On October 20, 2013, Kollab tweeted, "tell me what makes Israel's 'we must remain a Jewish state' obsession any less disturbing than Hitler's obsession with a pure white nation."

She also tweeted anti-Semitic conspiracies. They said Israel runs America and the "zionist-owned media."" She tweeted on February 27, 2013, "How can we be angry at misguided ppl in the West? The media and schools are the most powerful tools- both are full of Zionist propaganda."

Donald Ciota II: 5 Fast Facts You Need to Know

––––––––––––––––––––––––––––––––––––––––––––––––

2. The Cleveland Clinic Became Aware of Her Posts During the First Year of Her Residency & She Was Fired After an Investigation

Lara Kollab.

Cleveland Clinic issued a statement on its website on December 31 saying that Lara Kollab no longer works there. "Cleveland Clinic was recently made aware of comments posted to social media by a former employee. This individual was employed as a supervised resident at our hospital from July to September 2018. She is no longer working at Cleveland Clinic. In no way do these beliefs reflect those of our organization. We fully embrace diversity, inclusion and a culture of safety and respect across our entire health system," the statement said.

Canary Mission's Twitter says it first posted its "profile" of Kollab, with the anti-Semitic tweets, in March 2018. The Canary Mission tweeted its info on Kollab again on December 27. Mainstream media picked it up for the first time. It also went viral on social media, leading to the Cleveland Clinic's comment.

Cleveland Clinic issued a second statement on January 2. It clarified that Kollab was fired in September after the hospital learned of her social media posts.

"This individual was employed as a supervised, first-year resident at our hospital from July to September 2018. Upon learning of the social media post, we acted. We did an internal review and placed her on leave. Her departure was related to those posts and she has not worked at Cleveland Clinic since September. First-year residents must have multiple safeguards and direct supervision for patient care and prescribing medicine. In addition, there have been no reports of any patient harm related to her work during the time she was here," Cleveland Clinic said in the statement. "In no way do these beliefs reflect those of our organization. We fully embrace diversity, inclusion and a culture of safety and respect across our entire health system."

---

### 3. Kollab Graduated From Touro College of Osteopathic Medicine, a School With Jewish Roots, Which Says It's 'Shocked' by Her Statements

Kollab graduated from Touro College of Osteopathic Medicine in New York in 2017, a school with Jewish roots. The campus she attended is located in Middletown, New York. The school's first class graduated in 2011 after it opened with an emphasis on training minority doctors.

"When we welcomed our first class in 2007, we had a rare opportunity. Touro's website says, "We imagined a program that embraced the new millennium's tech and medical standards. It would be socially aware." "Touro College of Osteopathic Medicine trains osteopathic physicians. It focuses on serving underserved communities and increasing underrepresented minorities in medicine." We value and support public service, research, and community health. We aim to improve health through graduate medical education and osteopathic work. We will educate students using the latest, innovative techniques. We will test them with summative and formative measures. Our goal is to graduate qualified osteopathic physicians."

Touro College was founded in New York City in 1971 and is the largest private Jewish university in the country.

After learning of the Twitter posts made by Kollab, Touro issued a statement on Twitter. "Touro College is appalled by anti-Semitic comments reportedly made by Lara Kollab, a graduate of its osteopathic medicine program." "The mission of Touro College is to educate, perpetuate, and enrich the historic Jewish tradition of tolerance and dignity," it said.

Before working at Cleveland Clinic, Kollab was at Loyola University Medical Center in Chicago. She was a fourth-year medical student at Touro in 2017.

Read More From Heavy

Tony Albert: 5 Fast Facts You Need to Know

----------------------------------------------

4. She Is an Ohio Native & Attended John Carroll University for Her Undergraduate Studies

Lara Kollab.

Lara Kollab, who said on social media that she is Muslim, is a native of Westlake, Ohio, according to public records. Kollab said on social media that she has worked as a tutor for high school and college students in her hometown, mentoring aspiring doctors.

Her now-deleted Linkedin profile says she attended John Carroll University in University Heights, Ohio, near Cleveland. She studied biology, neuroscience and psychology while at John Carroll with a goal of attending medical school after graduation, according to her social media posts. She finished her studies at John Carroll in 2013, according to her Facebook page. Some of the Twitter posts were made while Kollab was a student at John Carroll. The university, a private Jesuit school, has not commented about the controversy.

Kollab said on Linkedin that since 2015, she has been a mentor to "1st, 2nd, and 3rd year medical students."

According to her now-deleted website, Kollab was a "internal medicine resident" and was based in Cleveland at the time of her firing. She wrote on the website, "at the heart of all Kollab does is a deep commitment to providing exceptional medical services to people in need of care."

Kollab wrote, "Her past work shows her passion to help underserved areas." She has provided medical services at a free clinic in a war-torn community at the Askar Refugee Camp, one of the largest refugee camps in the Middle East. She has also been part of a Global Brigades Medical Mission to Honduras."

She wrote on the website, "When not practicing medicine, Kollab enjoys cooking Middle Eastern food, learning about cultures, traveling, writing, and photography.""

---------------------------------------------------

5. Kollab's Training Certificate With the Ohio Medical Board Was Issued in July 2018 & Remains Active Until June 2021

Lara Kollab.

Dr. Lara Kollab still has an active training certificate with the Ohio medical board, a search on the state's medical license lookup shows. She was granted the training certificate on July 24, 2018, and it was effective as of July 1 of that same year. The certificate is set to expire on June 30, 2021. The license search website shows that the board has not take any action against her.

According to the website, "The Joint Commission and NCQA consider on-line status information as fulfilling the primary source verification requirement for verification of licensure in compliance with their respective credentialing standards."

Tessie Pollock, the licensing board's communications director, told Fox News, "Her certificate is valid as long as the individual is actively part of the program, as indicated on the training certificate application by the supervising entity."" Pollock added, "The Ohio Medical Board's mission is to protect the health and safety of all Ohioans." Malicious acts and attitudes toward any population go against the Medical Practices Act and are denounced by the board."

## Part B

### ANOTHER Muslim Doctor saying he would kill Jewish patients

By <u>Pamela Geller</u> - on October 16, 2021

<u>ISLAMIC JEW HATRED</u>

<u>Jew hatred</u> is a central tenet of Islam. Until these genocidal calls are condemned, Islamic terrorism will rise. Its body count will grow.

<u>Imam: Quran Focuses On Jews So Much Because They Are Our Sworn Enemy With Whom We Can Never Make Peace</u>

<u>More on Muslim doctors.</u>…..

<u>More on Islamic Jew hatred</u>

Related:

<u>Muslim Doctor who made DEADLY threats against Jews requests hearing before State Medical Board of Ohio</u>

<u>Muslim Doctor Subjected to Hate Campaign by Muslim Jew-Haters Over Charity Work With Jews</u>

<u>Cleveland: Antisemitic Muslim Doctor Lara Kollab, "I'll purposely give Jews the wrong meds"</u>

<u>Phoenix Children's Hospital: Muslim Doctor Who Accused Jewish State of Cannibalism</u>

<u>Muslima Pediatric Radiologist Dr. Fidaa Wishah Accuses Jews of Cannibalism, Calls for End to Jewish State</u>

<u>Tufts Muslim Dental Students Horrific Antisemitic Tweets Uncovered</u>

NY Hospital Trying to Fire Antisemitic Doctor Walid Khass Who Calls for Jewish Blood and Violence Against Jews

Ohio: Muslim Dentist Nessreen Zayed Supports Genocide of Jews Wants to Torture 'Zionist' Patients

Ohio Jew-hating Muslim Dr. Lara Kollab who was fired for deadly threats against Jews given residency in California

Trump lawyer: Genocidal Muslim doctor Lara Kollab must be banned for life

Hassan Hammo, a clean cut Jordanian doctor is currently doing his residency in Internal Medicine at Cook County Health in Chicago.

Would you want to know if the Doctor you were entrusting with your care tweeted about stabbing Jews? Meet Hasan Abdelhail Hammo – currently doing his residency in Internal Medicine at

@CookCtyHealth

@CookCountyIMR

طيب ممكن و احنا بنقصف نميل على اليهود من مرة؟ يعني كونهم العدو الاول في المنطقة؟

Translated from Arabic by Google

Ok, is it possible that we bombard the Jews once? Does it mean that they are the number one enemy in the region?

ترى الجلي مش صعب، و مرات بكون حلو، بس الله يخرب بيت اليهود ما اكثره

Translated from Arabic by Google

You see, the clear is not difficult, and sometimes it is sweet, but God destroys the Jews' house, how much is it?

Antisemitic medical student, Abdulazeez (Abood) Swaiti, was reportedly kicked out of Brody School of Medicine for racist tweets.

Israeli Cool  Another case of old tweets coming back to haunt you, because even though you delete them, they never really go away.

Abdulazeez (Abood) Swaiti, a student at East Carolina University's Brody School of Medicine, had a bad case of Jew hatred. According to commenter ECU, who is a student at ECU's health science campus, he was dismissed from the medical school soon after his tweets were found.

Looks like he has a problem with Black people and Asians, as well.

**Abood Swaiti** @Aboo... · 2012-05-23 ···
never in my life will an asian have my vote

💬 2    ↻    ♡    ⬆

**Abood Swaiti** @Aboo... · 2012-06-16 ···
Replying to @StayDank_

@StayDank_ @ohmy_allah lol shutup you
dirty nigger! Yea that's right I said that
shit on twitta

💬 1    ↻    ♡    ⬆

**Abood Swaiti** @Aboo... · 2013-05-08 ···
@LifeAsNura NIGGER I'M TOO BUZY
FOR U

💬    ↻    ♡    ⬆

**Abood Swaiti** @Aboo... · 2013-01-08 ···
Replying to @JuicyJoee

@JuicyJoee bruh I fuck wit egypt as a
country but all its ppl r some dirty
niggers. Except dor u n morsi yall my
niggas

(Note: The word for "BLACK" in Arabic is Same Word for Slave-
Glen R. Cook)

Part C

**Debbie Schlussel May 17, 2007, - 5:01 am**
<u>**When Your Doctor is a Muslim: Medical Terrorism Comes to America**</u>

By **** **IMPORTANT UPDATE, 07/05/07: Please read my 07/03/07** **** Sometimes–so many times–diversity is not what it's cracked up to be. Just ask <u>Joseph Applebaum</u>. Well, you could ask him. But you won't get an answer. He's dead. And he's dead because he was a Jew, and his doctor is a Muslim and grad of "Ayman Al-Zawahiri" Medical School. But Applebaum wasn't denied treatment for being a Jew in Egypt. Or elsewhere in the Muslim world. It happened right here on U.S. soil. In Chicago. As lax immigration laws let in many Muslim doctors, hospitals have hired some. Many hospitals in the Detroit area are now dominated by Muslim doctors and have been for some time.

**Joseph Applebaum, *Z"L*\*: Muslim Doctor Refused to Treat Him, Let Him Die**

But, even in hospitals where they are not the majority, Muslim doctors are starting to show alarming behavior toward non-Muslim patients. On December 1, 2003, Joe Applebaum was admitted to Rush North Shore Medical Center, a major hospital in Chicago. He was stricken with an acute (or distended) abdomen–a swelling of the stomach that is easily diagnosed and treated. But it was never treated by anyone at the hospital. For 12 hours, Joe Applebaum was left alone–left to die, which he did the next day. A Jewish man, he was identified as a Jew on the front page of his medical chart. Dr. Osama Ahmed Ibrahim, the chief resident, noticed a religious note on Mr. Applebaum's chart. And it appears that this is why he never once checked or examined this emergency patient, Mr. Applebaum, and left him to die. When another doctor at the hospital finally examined Mr. Applebaum, he told his son, Michael, to say goodbye. His father was about to die. Dr. Ibrahim, is a Muslim from Birmingham, England–a hotbed of Islamic radicalism and terror planning. It is breeding ground for anti-Semitic hate. He is a graduate of Ain Shams University Medical School in Egypt. This extremist school featured on its faculty the father of Al-Qaeda mastermind and number two, Dr. Ayman Al-Zawahiri. Pere Zawahiri was a Muslim Brotherhood activist. Other Ain Shams faculty members and grads include:

* late HAMAS leader Sheikh Ahmed Yassin; * Muslim Brotherhood President Mohammed Mahdi Akef; * LAX terrorist shooter Hesham Mohamed Hedayet; * Extremist Canadian Imam, Aly Hindy; and * Co-leader of Yemen's extremist Al-Islah Party, Abdul Majeed Al-Zindani.

Why did Dr. Ibrahim neglect a patient who came in with an easily treatable condition and leave him to die, 12 hours later? It appears it can only be because he did not want to treat a Jewish patient and let him live. There can be no other reason. Mr. Applebaum's son, Michael, is a medical doctor and an attorney. While waiting for Dr. Ibrahim to see his father, he called the doctor. He wanted to alert him to his father's worsening condition and acute abdomen. Dr. Ibrahim claimed he examined Mr. Applebaum. But that was a lie. He'd never seen him. And he essentially murdered him by denying treatment. It's a case of extreme negligence and medical malpractice for the apparent purpose of anti-Semitic murder. Joseph Applebaum's son Michael is now suing Dr. Ibrahim, the hospital–Rush North Shore Medical Center, and others involved in his father's murder. The case is filed in Illinois, and he is looking for a good attorney to pursue the case he has filed. If you are interested or can help, please contact him at the website he set up to document this ongoing tragedy. This isn't the only case where a Muslim doctor deliberately let his Jewish patient die, it is just the first that we know of. And it likely won't be the last. Many Muslim doctors, especially those from foreign medical schools, hold anti-Semitic, anti-American views. This includes some from here, too. Their backgrounds are incompatible with the basic level of care required and expected in America. Sadly, no-one is vetting them out of our healthcare system. And no-one will. But we know that there are many doctors who've been at the forefront of taking lives–not saving them–in the name of the "Religion of Peace":

\* Dr. Ayman Al-Zawahiri–Al-Qaeda mastermind and number two man, reportedly a surgeon and/or psychiatrist; \* Dr. Mohammad Rabi Al-Zawahiri–Ayman's father and a Muslim Brotherhood enthusiast, pharmacologist and professor at Ain Shams Medical School; \* Dr. "Abu Hafiza"–Al-Qaeda master planner who was the brains and commander of the Moroccan cell that provided logistics for the 9/11 attacks, and he recruited Qaeda insurgents for battles in Fallujah, Moroccan psychiatrist; \* Dr. Abdel Aziz Al-Rantisi–Late HAMAS leader, pediatrician; \* Dr. Mahmoud Al-Zahar–HAMAS co-founder and leader, surgeon and lecturer at the Islamic University in Gaza; \* Dr. Fathi Abd Al-Aziz Shiqaqi–Late founder of Islamic Jihad and active in Fatah, physician; \* Dr. George Habash–Founder and chief of the Popular Front for the Liberation of Palestine (PFLP), pediatrician (which is interesting since he rocketed a school bus full of children in Avivim, Israel; \* Dr. Bashar Assad–President of Terror-sponsor state Syria, welcoming home to every Islamic terrorist group imaginable, ophthalmologist.

And there are other issues, such as infectious disease. We are seeing cases in Britain where some Muslim doctors refuse to use alcohol-based hand sanitizer. They are prohibited from consuming alcohol in their faith. In New Jersey, , a Muslim Arab resident, severed and stole the hand of a cadaver as a gift for a stripper. Such little respect for life from a religion now very much participating in a profession that takes an oath to do no harm and to preserve patient's lives. He got a slap on the hand. No jail time, likely no record. He now practices medicine at Maimonides Medical Center in New York. The real Maimonides–a legendary, brilliant Jewish doctor, rabbi, and religious scholar–is turning over in his grave. Dr. Applebaum's suit against Rush North Shore may make hospitals wary of hiring Muslim doctors who practice medical terrorism. Today, the victim is a Jew, solely because he is Jewish. But tomorrow, it will be a Christian, solely because he/she is a Christian. Or some other non-Muslim victim, solely because he/she is a non-Muslim victim. Can we afford doctors in America? Their loyalty to patients is less than their extreme devotion to a hateful religion. If they cannot and will not tender care, they should not be licensed to practice medicine in the United States. Like I said, Maimonides is turning over in his grave. Joseph Applebaum, *Zichrono LiVrachah*–Blessed Be His Memory.

BARE NAKED ISLAM
ENEMYWITHIN-AMERICA

ISLAM IN AMERICA

ISLAMIZATION OF THE WEST

ENEMYWITHIN-FOREIGN

ISLAM AND THE JEWS

ISLAMIC BRITAIN

CAIR NAZIS

MUSLIM INVADERS

RELIGION OF HATE

WOMEN
YET ANOTHER reason for Americans never to use a Muslim doctor (barenakedislam.com)

**YET ANOTHER reason for Americans never to use a Muslim doctor**

NOVEMBER 11, 2019 BY BARENAKEDISLAM

VIRGINIA: A Pakistani Muslim fertility doctor's 'demographic jihad' included unauthorized surgeries on non-Muslim women, Feds say. He tied their fallopian tubes and performed hysterectomies without consent.

*Javaid Perwaiz, 69, of Chesapeake (Western Tidewater Regional Jail)*

<u>PJ Media</u> The details of this case are simply horrifying. One woman tried for years to conceive a child, but couldn't. After finally seeing a fertility specialist, she learned, per the Virginian-Pilot, that her «Fallopian tubes had been burned down to nubs, making it impossible to conceive naturally.»"

It turned out that her Muslim physician, Dr. Javaid Perwaiz, of Chesapeake, Virginia, a native of Pakistan, had tied her tubes without telling her was doing it or obtaining her consent. And she was by no means the only woman whom Dr. Perwaiz victimized in this way.

## 6.4. What is Demographic Jihad?

Demographic Jihad is the act of helping a minority ethnic population increase itself within a country to alter the social and/or political norms of that country.

Three typical methods:
1. High minority-group immigration rates.
2. Higher-than-normal minority-group birth rates.
3. Lower-than-normal host-group birthrates.
[http://en.wikipedia.org/wiki/Demographic_threat]

11/8/2013     Mohammed-and-Political-Islam-is-it-something-we-should-worry-about-Rev2.ppl     39

*Dr. Perwaiz's website is very helpful. It says he has "practiced in the Chesapeake region for over 30 years, providing expert and individualized care to his patients.""*

*He follows each patient throughout their pregnancy. He is available 24/7 to meet all your requests and expectations. His experienced office staff will individualize your care and coordinate your insurance coverage. They provide friendly and knowlegable service for all your healthcare needs. Same day appointments are often available.*

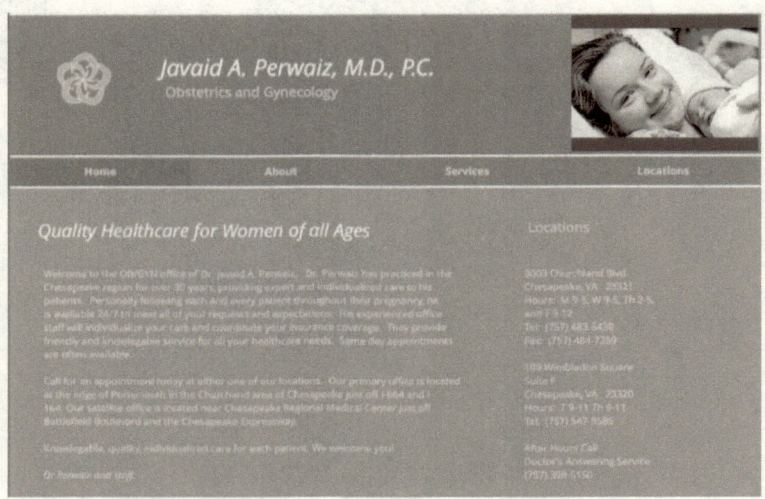

We are told the good doctor was "educated abroad," with no hint as to where. It was in his native Pakistan. The Virginian-Pilot notes: "Perwaiz has had a medical license since at least 1980, according to state records. He attended medical school in Pakistan and completed a residency at Charleston Area Medical Center."

Dr. Perwaiz was arrested Friday. He faces trial for health care fraud and for making false statements about health care." A local hospital employee tipped off the FBI fourteen months ago. They suspected he was performing unnecessary surgeries on patients who didn't know the procedures.

The offices of Dr. Javaid Perwaiz, located at 3003 Churchland Blvd. in Chesapeake. (Google Street View)

*According to the Virginian-Pilot, "the employee told investigators Perwaiz's patients advised hospital staff they were there for their 'annual clean outs,' according to an affidavit signed by FBI Special Agent Desiree Maxwell."*

*These "annual clean outs" consisted of "hysterectomies, cystectomies, myomectomies, tubal ligation and dilation & curettage," and more. He was busy, too: "From January 2014 to August 2018, he performed a surgical procedure on 40 percent of his Medicaid patients — 510 in all. Of those, 42 percent underwent two or more surgeries."*

*This isn't the first time we've seen this. In Sri Lanka, a Muslim doctor was accused of sterilizing non-Muslim patients without their knowledge or consent. It was called "Population Jihad." The doctor sterilized thousands of non-Muslim mothers. A Muslim doctor sterilized thousands of Hindu and Buddhist women during cesarean surgeries.*

We have 50 million Muslims in Europe. There are signs that Allah will grant Islam victory in Europe—without swords, without guns, without conquest—will turn it into a Muslim continent within a few decades.

(Muammar Gaddafi)

*Also, consider this. In 1974, Algeria's president, Houari Boumedienne, said at the UN: "One day, millions will leave the Southern Hemisphere for the North."" And they will not go there as friends. Because they will go there to conquer it. And they will conquer it with their sons. The wombs of our women will give us victory."*

*A representative of the Iranian army, Abbas Mohammad Hassani, said: "In the current circumstances, childbearing is a type of jihad. It would please the Almighty God."*

Look what has happened to the Michigan city of Hamtramck, formerly a city of Polish immigrants, now a Muslim majority city.

RELATED STORIES/VIDEOS:

**WHAT WERE YOU THINKING? Of all the good doctors in America you could choose, you chose a Muslim one?**

**ONE MORE REASON never to allow a Muslim doctor to touch you**

**NEVER USE A MUSLIM DOCTOR, EITHER**

**NEVER BE TREATED BY A MUSLIM DOCTOR, either**

**NEVER use a Muslim doctor…especially if you are Jewish**

**Apparently, her problems didn't end after the Muslim doctor, Lara Kollab, who threatened to give "Jewish patients the wrong meds" was fired from the Cleveland Clinic**

Yet another reason for Jews to avoid ever being treated by any Muslim doctor, anywhere!

The problem isn't that your Muslim doctor might be a jihadist, it's that you're using a Muslim doctor

YET ANOTHER MUSLIM doctor and his wife arrested in Michigan for performing Female Genital Mutilation on young girls

Part D

# ISIS DOCTORS Part A

**Witnesses Accuse British ISIS Doctors of Carrying
Out 'Nazi-Style' Experiments on Prisoners
By Andrew J. Sciascia April 27, 2019 at 3:04pm The Western Journal**

Syrian eyewitnesses report that two British healthcare workers, who joined the Islamic State, are torturing captives with "Nazi-style" medical experiments.

A 10-man medical team worked in a hospital in eastern Syria. It was reported that they were harvesting organs from prisoners. They were using the organs to implant in injured jihadists or selling them on the black market. They also conducted chemical experiments on human subjects and tortured people psychologically.

The Islamic State "health minister" allegedly leading the medical team is a former British NHS doctor, Issam Abuanza.

A 40-year-old Sheffield native, Abuanza left his wife and kids to join the Islamic State in 2014. He quickly rose to a high rank in the group, the Daily Mail reported.

British intelligence reports that, since 2006, the doctor had been discontented with his job. He began espousing radical views online and at work, claiming the NHS treated its doctors in a subhuman manner.

Abuanza was later found to be posting disturbing comments online about the Islamic State captives executed in viral videos in the early 2010s.

Still, Abuanza was able to secure work in the United Kingdom until his departure in 2014.

Aghiad al-Kheder, co-founder of Sound and Picture, spoke to the Daily Mail on Friday. The group seeks to expose the human rights abuses of Islamic extremists in the region. He said the "Islamic State needed to show it was a government, not a radical group, so it appointed a minister for everything.""

"Issam was minister for health which meant he was responsible for everything health related," al-Kheder said.

Al-Kheder also told Daily Mail that even Islamic State jihadists he had spoken to reported being disgusted with Abuanza's medical torture techniques, referring to them as "brutal," "Nazi-style" experiments.

One jihadi who spoke with al-Kheder spoke of undisclosed chemical materials being used on helpless captors. He also reported mutilated corpses being left in cells with live prisoners.

"They experimented with torture and with chemical materials but we were not sure for what purposes." he said.

"They used the materials on the prisoners."

The Daily Mail says, the other British healthcare worker on Abuanza's team was Mohammad Anwar Miah, a former pharmacist. He aided organ removal and transplant.

Miah, captured by Syrian Democratic Forces earlier this year, called those reports false in a February interview with the Daily Mail.

In his interview, Miah claimed he had been working as a doctor giving "humanitarian aid" in Mayadin, Syria. Miah also says he never contacted other British healthcare workers in Syria. He was largely unaware of Islamic State fighters torturing and publicly executing people in the city.

Miah has asked to be sent back to the UK. He claims he is not "a danger to the public." He will join "any rehabilitation program" the government requires.

"I came here to do humanitarian work, I came here with that intention and that's what I did. I didn't have any political or military involvement. I did not take part in any of these atrocities or incited any hatred or made any videos. I have never killed or hurt anybody," Miah said.

As of this report, Miah had not been released to the United Kingdom, and Abuanza was reported to be hiding out in caves near Baghouz.

**ISIS Part B**

**ISIS 'doctors' harvesting healthy prisoners' ORGANS and using them as living bloodbank**

**ISLAMIC State doctors are harvesting healthy captives' organs and draining their blood, according to a former prisoner.**

**By JAKE BURMAN 00:00, Thu, Oct 1, 2015 | UPDATED: 09:08, Thu, Oct 1, 2015 UK EXPRESS**

ISIS doctors are allegedly harvesting prisoners' organs

Abo Rida, an escaped prisoner, claimed that surgeons for a brutal terror group removed prisoners' kidneys and corneas. They also used them as "blood banks" for injured militants.

Rida also disclosed that ISIS militants in Raqqa tortured prisoners who weren't strong enough to donate organs. Raqqa is the regime's Syrian stronghold.

He said the situation inside their make-shift prisons is getting "worse day after day".

ISIS supporters wave the terror group's flag

ISIS was using them as a blood bank to withdraw blood when they need it for injured members

Abo Rida

Rida, who escaped the abhorrent terrorists, said militants gave "special care" to healthy prisoners. They escaped after a day of horrific torture.

He said: "ISIS was using them as a blood bank to withdraw blood when they need it for injured members."

The former prisoner escaped a group four months ago. A counter-terrorism raid directly hit the prison he was in. The dust it created let him sneak out.

He also revealed how the shameless doctors for the terror regime harvested their captives' organs.

Islamic State 'selling off the organs of women kept as sex slaves...

French train gunman linked to ISIS claims he 'FOUND AK-47 and...

Rida said the doctors "moved organs such as kidneys and corneas from the prisoners" because their fate was "inevitable death".

He claimed the terror group believed the jihadists were "more deserving" of the organs.

Rida said that, after being accused of crimes, prisoners with him endured "all kinds of torture." They were accused of insulting Allah, trying to topple the jihadists, and being part of the free army.

An escaped prisoner claimed surgeons drain prisoners' blood for fighters

He said the savage torture would last all day with no "specific time" for it to start and finish.

The escaped prisoner was one of only four detainees who managed to make it to safety.

He said: "Not many of us could escape because ISIS members fired at us."

Rida said the doctors even drained prisoners of blood

It is not the first time ISIS has been accused of harvesting organs. Earlier this year, the UN was urged to investigate the terror group's trade in human organs in Iraq.

Iraqi ambassador Mohamed Alhakim claimed that dozens of bodies with surgical incisions and missing parts have been found in shallow mass graves near Mosul.

**Mr Alhakim said: "We have bodies. Come and examine them. It is clear they are missing certain parts."**

RELATED ARTICLES

ISIS threat to UK hospitals: Terrorists 'could hijack and pump LETHAL drugs into patients'

**ISIS Part C**

**Pakistani doctor arrested in Minnesota on terrorism charge**

**A Pakistani doctor and former researcher at the Mayo Clinic in Rochester, Minnesota, has been arrested on a terrorism charge**

**By AMY FORLITI Associated Press March 19, 2020, 8:01 PM**

MINNEAPOLIS -- A Pakistani doctor and former Mayo Clinic research coordinator was arrested Thursday in Minnesota on a terrorism charge, after prosecutors say he told paid FBI informants that he had pledged his allegiance to the Islamic State group and wanted to carry out lone wolf attacks in the United States.

FBI agents arrested Muhammad Masood, 28, at the Minneapolis-St. Paul Airport on Thursday. He was charged with trying to support a foreign terrorist organization.

Prosecutors say Masood was in the U.S. on a work visa. They allege that, starting in January, Masood made several statements to paid informants. He believed they were members of the Islamic State group. In these statements, he pledged his allegiance to the group and its leader. **He also allegedly expressed his desire to travel to Syria to fight for ISIS and a desire to carry out lone wolf attacks in the U.S.**

At one point, Masood messaged an informant "there is so much I wanted to do here .. .lon wulf stuff you know ... but I realized I should be on the ground helping brothers sisters kids," according to an FBI affidavit.

Prosecutors say Masood bought a plane ticket on Feb. 21 to travel from Chicago to Amman, Jordan, and then planned to go to Syria from there. He had planned to leave at the end of March. But on March 16, he had to change his travel plans because Jordan closed its borders due to the coronavirus pandemic. Masood and an informant then made a plan. He would fly from Minneapolis to Los Angeles to meet the informant. Masood believed the informant would help him travel by cargo ship into Islamic State territory.

Masood was arrested Thursday at the airport after he checked in for his flight to Los Angeles. His attorney, Manny Atwal, had no immediate comment.

Court documents do not name the clinic where Masood worked. But, a LinkedIn page for a man with the same name and work history says Masood has worked at the Mayo Clinic in Rochester, Minnesota, since February 2018. He was a research trainee, but has been a clinical research coordinator since May. A profile on researchgate.net says he has done research in cardiology. An online calendar of the event says he was to present his research for the Mayo Clinic School of Continuous Professional Development in October 2018.

Mayo Clinic spokeswoman Ginger Plumbo said Masood formerly worked there. But, "he was not employed by Mayo Clinic at the time of his arrest." An affidavit supporting the complaint said Masood planned to notify his employer that his last day of work would be March 17.

The affidavit said the FBI began investigating in January. Someone, later found to be Masood, had posted messages on an encrypted social media platform. They indicated an intent to support ISIS.

On Jan. 24, Masood messaged an informant on an encrypted app. He said he was a doctor with a Pakistani passport. He wanted to travel to Syria, Iraq, or northern Iran to fight on the front lines and help the wounded, the affidavit said.

He explained that he wanted to make the trip because he "hates smiling at the passing kuffar just to not make them suspicios." The affidavit said kuffar is an Arabic term meaning nonbeliever or non-Muslim. Masood also allegedly told the informant he wanted help getting to the front lines. When the informant said Masood might have to kill people, Masood replied, "i want to kill and get killed ... and kill and get killed."

Once, the informant set up a video call with the second informant. Masood believed he was an overseas commander who could vet him to fight for ISIS. Masood allegedly told that informant he wanted to be a combat medic and fight, and had been ready to go for some time.

Since 2007, about three dozen Minnesotans, mostly Somali men, have left to join al-Shabab in Somalia or Islamic State militants in Syria. Several others were convicted for plotting to join or support those groups. The charges were terrorism-related.

———

Follow Amy Forliti on Twitter: https://www.twitter.com/amyforliti

# Stop Foreign funding for Mosques

**Denmark Bans Foreign Funding of Mosques
by Soeren Kern March 15, 2021 at 5:00 am
Note: This has just happened in Texas funded
by Indonesia>- Glen R. Cook**

"The mosque is a gift from Qatar but it's not free. I have always said that they will expect something in return, and this shows that they are making some claims for their money." — Lars Aslan Rasmussen, Copenhagen city councilman.

Officials from almost all of Denmark's main political parties support a bill to ban foreign funding of mosques.

"It is a real problem if donations are made from organizations that want to undermine fundamental democratic values." — Foreign Affairs Minister Mattias Tesfaye.

Denmark's first purpose-built mosque, the Grand Mosque of Copenhagen, opened in June 2014. It is also called the Hamad Bin Khalifa Civilization Center. The former emir of Qatar, Hamad bin Khalifa al Thani, donated 227 million Danish kroner (€30 million; $36 million) for it. Pictured: Qatar's Minister of Religious Affairs, Ghaith bin Mubarak Ali Omran Al-Kuwari (second from left), at the Grand Mosque of Copenhagen's opening on June 19, 2014. (Photo by Thomas Lekfeldt/AFP via Getty Images)

The Danish Parliament has approved a new law that bans foreign governments from financing mosques in Denmark. The measure aims to stop Muslim countries, especially Qatar, Saudi Arabia, and Turkey, from promoting Islamic extremism in Danish mosques and prayer facilities.

Denmark joins a growing list of European countries. They include Austria, Belgium, France, Germany, Italy, the Netherlands, and Switzerland. These countries have acted to stop foreign governments from funding the building and upkeep of mosques on their lands.

Recently, Algeria, Kuwait, Libya, Morocco, Saudi Arabia, Turkey, Qatar, and the UAE donated hundreds of millions of euros to spread Islam in Europe.

On March 9, the Danish Parliament voted 79 to 7 to approve Act 81, "Proposal for a Law Prohibiting Donations from Certain Persons." The law does not name Islam or Islamism. It states:

"The purpose of the Act is to prevent natural and legal persons, including foreign state authorities and state-run organizations and companies, from working against or undermining democracy and fundamental freedoms and human rights by making donations.

"The Minister of Immigration and Integration Affairs may ... make a decision on whether natural and legal persons, including foreign state authorities and state-run organizations and companies that oppose or undermine democracy and fundamental freedoms and human rights, be placed on a public ban list....

"Anyone who receives one or more donations that individually or together exceed DKK 10,000 (€1,350; $1,600) within 12 consecutive calendar months, from a natural or legal person who is included on the public ban list ... is punishable by a fine.

"Anyone who ... has received one or more donations that individually or together exceed DKK 10,000 within 12 consecutive calendar months ... must return the donation to the donor within 14 days from the time when the person in question became or should have become aware of this...."

The legislation was sponsored by the Ministry of Foreign Affairs and Integration and enters into force on March 15, 2021. Foreign Minister Mattias Tesfaye said:

"Today there are extreme forces abroad that are trying to turn our Muslim citizens against Denmark and thus divide our society. Several times in recent years, the media have reported on Danish mosques receiving millions from the Middle East, among others. The government will oppose this.

"This bill is an important step towards fighting attempts by Islamic extremists to gain ground in Denmark. With this, we can take a targeted approach to the donations that undermine the values on which Danish society is based.

"The bill will not solve all the problems that extreme Islamists and anti-democratic forces can give rise to. But it is a good step on the road, and it will be a benefit to society every time we can stop an anti-democratic donation in Denmark."

Tesfaye took action after the Danish newspaper Berlingske reported in January 2020 that Saudi Arabia had donated 4.9 million Danish kroner (€660,000; $780,000) to fund the Taiba Mosque, located in the "multicultural" Nørrebro district, also known as "little Arabia." The donation was made by means of the Embassy of Saudi Arabia in Denmark.

The Taiba Mosque, one of the most conservative in Denmark, has been the base for a number of Islamists convicted of terrorism offenses.

The Taiba Mosque's annual report included the donation. It was the first proof that Saudi Arabia was donating to Danish mosques. Berlingske subsequently reported that Saudi Arabia was financing other mosques in Denmark.

Denmark's first purpose-built mosque, the Grand Mosque of Copenhagen, opened in June 2014. It is officially known as the Hamad Bin Khalifa Civilization Center. The former emir of Qatar, Hamad bin Khalifa al Thani, donated 227 million Danish kroner (€30 million; $36 million) to fund it.

Critics of the mega-mosque, which holds 3,000 indoors and 1,500 in a courtyard, said the Danish Islamic Council (DIR) was promoting a very conservative view of Islam.

In September 2013, the mosque was still under construction. The Copenhagen Post reported that it planned to rebroadcast Al-Aqsa TV, a Hamas-controlled channel. At the time, city councilman Lars Aslan Rasmussen, himself of Turkish background, said:

"A few weeks ago, Dansk Islamisk Råd said that there would be no connection to Qatar and we can now see that is a lie. The mosque is a gift from Qatar but it's not free. I have always said that they will expect something in return, and this shows that they are making some claims for their money. This will not be a moderate mosque and it will present integration problems."

Turkey has funded the building of 27 mosques in Denmark. These are in Aarhus, Ringsted, and Roskilde, and in Fredericia, Hedehusene, and Holbæk.

In September 2020, Berlingske reported that Abu Bashar, a notorious imam in Odense, forced a woman to sign a document. It stated she would lose custody of her children if she divorced her husband. He said that such a divorce would violate the family's honor.

The document, which contravened Danish law, caused alarm among Danish officials. Prime Minister Mette Frederiksen wrote:

"Sharia does not belong in Denmark. Yesterday and today, we have read about divorce contracts based on Sharia. On Funen [the third-largest island in Denmark]. In Denmark. It is wrong. It is oppressive of women. It is not Danish. And it must never, ever become Danish.

"In government, we will do everything in our power to stop this. An imam should not interfere in divorce at all. It is only a choice to be made by the two persons who entered into the marriage. Nobody else. This confirms our fearful suspicions about the undemocratic tendencies that exist in parts of Denmark.

"We will do everything we can to stop it."

Almost all of Denmark's main political parties support a bill to ban foreign funding of mosques. Foreign Affairs Minister Mattias Tesfaye said:

"I take a deep distance from the extreme forces in Danish mosques. It is a real problem if donations are made from organizations that want to undermine fundamental democratic values. That is why I am glad that there is broad political agreement on the main ideas in the forthcoming bill. The bill may not necessarily solve all problems, but it is an important step in the right direction."

Liberal Party rapporteur Mads Fuglede added:

"We must and must never find ourselves in the hands of anti-democratic forces trying to assert their influence in Denmark. That is why we in the Liberal Party are pleased. There is now broad support for the work we started in government. We have a political responsibility to take care of Denmark. And we do it best by preventing donations from dark forces that want to undermine our democracy."

Pia Kjærsgaard, co-founder of the Danish People's Party, said:

"Obviously, Middle Eastern regimes must not be able to send money to mosques or Koranic schools in Denmark to undermine Danish values. We welcome this intervention. We hope to curb attacks on democracy, especially those from radicalized mosques. We must never accept attacks on our peaceful society and democracy. So, I am pleased that the government has chosen to implement this agreement from before the election. I look forward to its effects."

Conservative Party spokesman Marcus Knuth, said:

"We support limits on foreign donations to religious groups that oppose our Danish values." We hope the work will boost efforts against extremist mosques and Islamist groups in Denmark."

Henrik Dahl of the Liberal Alliance stated:

"We want to ensure that in Denmark no financial support is provided from anti-democratic organizations and individuals. We do not want outsiders to undermine democracy, freedom and fundamental human rights, or to have any kind of influence in Denmark. That is what this bill helps to prevent."

Prime Minister Frederiksen recently said her government will limit asylum seekers in Denmark. The aim, she said, is to preserve "social cohesion" in the country.

Denmark, with 5.8 million people, received about 40,000 asylum applications in the past five years, according to Statista. Most of the applications received by Denmark, a predominately Lutheran country, were from migrants from Muslim countries in Africa, Asia and the Middle East.

In recent years, Denmark has also permitted significant non-asylum immigration, especially from non-Western countries. Denmark is now home to sizeable immigrant communities from Syria (35,536); Turkey (33,111); Iraq (21,840); Iran (17,195); Pakistan (14,471); Afghanistan (13,864); Lebanon (12,990) and Somalia (11,282), according to Statista.

Muslims currently comprise approximately 5.5% of the Danish population, according to the Pew Research Center. Under a "zero migration scenario," the Muslim population is projected to reach 7.6%

by 2050; with a "medium migration scenario," it is forecast to hit 11.9% by 2050; and under a "high migration scenario," Muslims are expected to comprise 16% of the Danish population by 2050, according to Pew.

As in other European countries, mass migration has resulted in increased crime and social tension. Danish cities have been plagued by shootings, car burnings and gang violence.

On January 22, during a hearing on Danish immigration policy, Frederiksen, a Social Democrat, said she wanted to reduce asylum approvals.

"Our goal is zero asylum seekers. We cannot promise zero asylum seekers, but we can establish the vision for a new asylum system, and then do what we can to implement it. We must be careful that not too many people come to our country, otherwise our social cohesion cannot exist. It is already being challenged."

Frederiksen, who has been prime minister since June 2019, also said that "politicians of the past" were "thoroughly wrong" for failing to insist that migrants must integrate into Danish society.

Soeren Kern is a Senior Fellow at the New York-based Gatestone Institute.

Note: Denmark joins a list of European countries. These include Austria, Belgium, France, Germany, Italy, the Netherlands, and Switzerland. They have all taken steps to prevent foreign governments from financing the building and upkeep of mosques. - Glen R. Cook

# Here is a list of 30 Locations Inside the United States of Islamic terrorist training camps.

1. Marion, Alabama 16. Hancock, New York (National Headquarters)
2. Baladullah, California 17. Talihina, Oklahoma
3. Oak Hill, California 18. Philadelphia, Pennsylvania
4. Squaw Valley, California 19. Saylorsburg, Pennsylvania
5. Tulare County, California 20. York, South Carolina
6. Buena Vista, Colorado 21 Dover, Tennessee
7. Tallahassee, Florida 22. Houston, Texas
8. Commerce, Georgia 23. Waco, Texas
9. Jessup, Georgia 24. Fairfax, Virginia
10. Springfield, Massachusetts 25. Falls Church, Virginia
11. Hagerstown, Maryland 26. Meherrin, Virginia
12. Hyattsville, Maryland 27. Red House, Virginia
13. Coldwater, Michigan 28. Roanoke, Virginia
14. Binghamton, New York 29. Bethany, West Virginia
15. Deposit, New York 30. Onalaska, Washington

Note : This list is dated and I have not been able to get a current one. – Glen R. Cook

# Islamist extremists hide huge stockpile of weapons near German mosque

**A HUGE stash of weapons reportedly belonging to Islamist extremists have been found hidden near a mosque in Germany.**
**By KATIE MANSFIELD**
**18:11, Wed, Jun 29, 2016 | UPDATED: 18:26, Wed, Jun 29, 2016**

The stockpile of weapons was found near a Mosque.

We use your sign-up to provide content in ways you've consented to and to improve our understanding of you. This may include adverts from us and 3rd parties based on our understanding. You can unsubscribe at any time. More info

The weapons arsenal was discovered during a top secret raid by a SWAT team in Nordrhein-Westfalen.

Local politician Ismail Tipi revealed details of the raid and warned of "the danger of fundamentalists".

The weapons were found in a cold room of a greengrocer near a mosque.

The state is the most populous state in Germany with nearly 18million people in the area, which includes Dusseldorf.

## RELATED ARTICLES

FEARS hundreds of ISIS terrorists could have snuck into Germany

**Terror threatened Germany plans to monitor 14-YEAR-OLD jihadis**

A weapons arsenal with war grade weapons was found in this search

Ismail Tipi

Mr Tipi, who is a member of the Hessian parliament, warned of the dangers of Salafi fundamentalists.

German officials said that the number of Salafist sympathizers has risen to 8,900, up from 7,000 in 2014. Salafists are ultra-conservative Islamists.

He said: "According to my information, a weapons arsenal with war grade weapons was found in this search."

"The danger of fundamentalist Salafists who are ready to use violence arming themselves in Germany is very large. This secret raid finding this weapons cache makes this more than clear."

Ismail Tipi raised concerns sleeper cells are gearing up for a terror attack on Germany

Three Syrian men were earlier this month suspected of planning large-scale attacks in Dusseldorf

Mr. Tipi, who received death threats for his anti-jihadi comments, warned that sleeper cells are planning a terror attack on Germany.

He said: "The information about this is increasing. There is a great fear that foreign hostile intelligence services support Salafist sleeper cells, jihadis, and ISIS terrorists in Germany.

"Through the weapons arsenal, the sleeper cells and militant jihadis can be armed with weapons and prepare for their likely attack. This is exactly what I have always feared."

He added: "Politicians must speak clearly about this.

## RELATED VIDEOS

Germany: Bavaria demands new criminal laws after Cologne NYE...

Cologne attacks: Algerian man acquitted of attempted sexual assault

Suspected Islamic State terrorists attack Istanbul Airport

"If these fears are true, we can assume that secret weapons are being readied for a major terrorist attack in Europe, including Germany." It would be a dereliction of duty if we didn't recognise this danger and find these weapons arsenals.

"We must see this danger and deal with it as soon as possible. Those in charge of our security must look at this closely and share this information with all relevant security agencies.

"Politicians must be clear. They must report possible dangers and threats. They should educate the public and urge vigilance. People must report all observations to the police." The problem of Salafism and IS-terrorism is always getting bigger when we don't react. Here everyone has a responsibility."

The German government is concerned that ISIS may increase attacks in Europe as it loses territory in Iraq and Syria. Its domestic intelligence agency is training to respond to a large-scale assault.

Interior Minister Thomas De Maiziere welcomed a US-led coalition's gains against ISIS in Iraq and Syria. But, he said, they did not reduce the risk of attacks in Europe.

He said: "On the contrary, we fear that Islamic State will shift its activities to Europe due to military losses in the region.""

Since the Paris attacks last November and Brussels in March, Germany has been on high alert for possible large-scale militant attacks, possibly involving military-style weapons.

Security chief Hans-George Maassen said the BfV had thwarted several attacks. It has also run drills to prepare for terrorism.

Three Syrian men were earlier this month suspected of planning large-scale attacks in Dusseldorf.

Mr. Maaseen said the agency was alert for lone-wolf attacks, self-radicalised individuals, and possible militants. These could be among the over one million refugees who entered Germany in the past year. He said authorities had found clear evidence against 17 individuals. They had entered Germany disguised as refugees. Most were either dead or had been arrested.

He said: "We must keep a particularly close eye on this group of people."

## TOOLS OF JIHAD

Shocking police photos reveal a 10,000-weapon arsenal. It includes howitzers, machine guns, and grenades for terrorists in Europe.

Police found the stash in Spain back in January but have only now released the terrifying images

By **Danny Collins**

**POLICE last night revealed an arsenal of more than 10,000 weapons destined for the hands of terrorists and organised gangs around Europe.**

A continent-wide operation stopped weapons from reaching extremists in France, Spain, and Belgium. These included anti-aircraft guns, howitzers, and grenades.

Some were previously described as being powerful enough to "bring down an aircraft".

A terrifying haul of more than 10,000 weapons has been revealed by continent-wide police force EuropolCredit: EPA

Investigators reckon the haul was for crime gangs and terrorists in Europe. Credit: EPA

Among the haul were automatic weapons, machine guns, howitzers and grenadesCredit: Getty Images

Europol announced the vast haul in January but only now have Spanish police published images of the devastating arsenal.

Among the stash were 10,000 rifles, 400 howitzers, anti-aircraft guns, grenades, pistols and revolvers.

Spanish cops also found a factory in Bilbao maintaining and reactivating old guns so they could be re-used.

Much of the cache is thought to have been bought legally through auctions before being reactivated.

They were then sold from the Spanish distribution centre which used a sports shop as its legal front.

Five people were arrested <u>following the raid back in January</u>.

A Europol statement said: "The seized weapons had an easy journey on the black market. They posed a significant risk of being acquired by organised crime groups and terrorists.""

Much of the haul had been purchased at auctions, reactivated and then sold via a warehouse in Bilbao, northern SpainCredit: EPA

Police found the stash in January but have only now released the terrifying imagesCredit: Getty Images

A probe into European gun runners was launched following an attack on Brussels' Jewish Museum in May 2014.

The attacker Mehdi Nemmouche was later arrested in Marseille, France, while carrying a Kalashnikov.

Following the original raid, Spanish police tweeted: "These are the 12,000 weapons, some capable of bringing down aircraft, intercepted from organised crime."

In November 2015, <u>Islamic extremists wielding automatic rifles similar to those seized killed 130 people in attacks on Paris</u>, including a bloody gun assault on the Bataclan theatre.

# First time in History

For the first time in history, a terrorist attack on the electric power grid has blacked-out an entire nation. Media has focused so much on the terror group ISIS. Their brutal conquest of northern Iraq and advance toward Baghdad drew attention. So, a perhaps greater threat, terrorists in Yemen, has been ignored.

**On June 9, Al Qaeda in the Arabian Peninsula (AQAP), used rocket propelled grenade launchers and mortars to destroy transmission towers, plunging the whole of Yemen into blackout. The AQAP blackout of Yemen's electric grid has gone largely unreported.**

Yemen, a nation of 24 million, is an important U.S. ally in the war on terrorism and has been the scene of some of the most significant episodes of that war. AQAP, based in Yemen, is notorious for its aggressive and ingenious terror operations against the United States.

On October 12, 2000, AQAP used explosives to turn a dinghy into a torpedo. It blasted the USS Cole, killing and injuring 56 sailors. The attack nearly sank the billion-dollar guided missile destroyer. The 9/11 Commission blamed the U.S. for not retaliating for the Cole. It said this led Al Qaeda to launch the 9/11 attacks, which killed 3,000 Americans.

AQAP has disguised bombs as soft drinks, underclothing, and printing cartridges. It wants to smuggle explosives aboard U.S.-bound airliners.

Last year, the Obama Administration evacuated U.S. embassies across the Middle East. This was in response to a plot by AQAP, involving coordinated activity by terror groups throughout the region.

On August 2, 2013, officials disclosed that, days earlier, the U.S. intercepted Al Qaeda leaders' communications. They indicated a major, imminent threat to U.S. interests in the Middle East and North Africa.

The State Department announced an "orderly downsizing," an evacuation, of two dozen embassies and diplomatic missions. The unprecedented evacuation included facilities in Egypt, Iraq, Kuwait, Saudi Arabia, Israel, and Yemen.

According to the Obama Administration, last year's terrorist teleconference was attended by more than 20 leaders of Al Qaeda and affiliates participating from the Middle East and North Africa. The conference included Al Qaeda members like Boko Haram, the Pakistani Taliban, Al Qaeda in Iraq, Al Qaeda in the Islamic Maghreb, and Al Qaeda in Uzbekistan. One intelligence officer reportedly described the gathering as "a legion of doom".

At the terror conference, Al Qaeda leader al-Zawahiri promoted AQAP's leader Nasir al-Wuhayshi to "Ma'sul al-Amm," or "General Manager" of Al Qaeda.

**The full objectives of last year's terror plot are unknown, but one goal included the takeover of Yemen.** Terrorists, disguised as Yemeni soldiers, were allegedly in position. They were ready to attack and seize military bases across Yemen.

**Why Yemen? North Korea may have supplied Yemen with at least 15 Scud-B missiles. They can deliver a one-ton warhead, with a 300 km range. The warhead may be nuclear, chemical, biological, or high-explosive. Iran has demonstrated that Scud missiles can be ship-launched from a freighter.**

The Obama Administration claimed it foiled a major terror plot. It cited its embassy evacuations and public warnings to allies. Since nothing much happened, it felt vindicated. Some analysts, including myself, criticized the Administration for disclosing sources and methods, making it more likely that the U.S. and allies would be surprised the next time.

Is it possible that the big terror offensive now rolling across the Middle East is the unfolding of the plot planned last year? **Media reporting acts as if the ISIS conquest of northern Iraq, Taliban attacks on nuclear-armed Pakistan, and the terror blackout in Yemen are unrelated. But all of these actors were plotting something together last year.**

Worry most about the Yemen nationwide blackout--which tomorrow could be the United States.

**A study by the U.S. Federal Energy Regulatory Commission found that** *attacks on just nine key transformer substations could blackout the entire nation for weeks or months.* **The Congressional Electromagnetic Pulse (EMP) Commission warned that** *a nuclear Scud missile launched from a freighter could blackout the U.S. for a year or more, killing up to 9 of 10 Americans by starvation and societal collapse.*

Yemen is yet another warning to protect the U.S. electric grid.

Dr. Peter Vincent Pry is Executive Director of the Task Force on National and Homeland Security, a Congressional Advisory Board. He served on the Congressional EMP Commission, the Strategic Posture Commission, the House Armed Services Committee, and the CIA. He is the author of Apocalypse Unknown and Electric Armageddon, both available on CreateSpace.com and Amazon.com.

# Hateful Targets

### by Glen Cook

There is no Collateral Damage in Islam

Continually throughout the world there is found child soldiers. This is particularly true in Africa and Southeast Asia. Many times, these children are kidnapped from their parents, extended families and clans. The issues are when the child is raised to be a suicide bomber or jihadist.

The real question becomes can that child, mosque, and school be considered a legitimate target. The answer, horrifying to western beliefs and philosophies has to be a strong and unwavering yes.

Recently, the Afghanistan government rescued forty-one children from Taliban extremist. Then the government had to find two ten year old boys who had entered Kabul to plan an attack. The government managed to locate them before the children put their attack into operation.

Once more western philosophies have had to deal with the idea that non Judeo-Christian cultures see children as expendable assets. The first time this was encountered on a large scale was the Hitler Youth fighting in World War Two. This was followed by the wars of independence in Southeast Asia and the Korean Conflict with children carrying grenades. After Korea, the American Soldier faced a similar situation in Vietnam. Children, "want a shoe shine, G.I.," carried bombs in shoeboxes, and worse. The next major war has been in Iraq and

Afghanistan. Once more, children are expendable. This was shown by the recent rescue and denial of forty-one "assets" by the Afghan government.

If a school is indoctrinating children to be suicide bombers, it is a valid target. It is the same as a bomb factory, munitions plant, training ground, or boot camp. By the same logic, a mosque would be a target. The Imam is urging parents to use their children in this way, and the parents agree. It would be better to destroy the Mosque and kill a small group than to let the Imam and the Mosque create a new terrorist every nine months. When children are kidnapped and indoctrinated in camps in Africa, then the camps must be targets, as well, for the same reason.

If we fail to stop children from becoming terrorists, we lose a generation. They will have no moral values or belief in the sanctity of life and family. Just look at the psychological profiles of the child "warriors" in Africa as they mature. As adults, they will have the same moral code.

For the western governments to maintain that Children cannot be a viable target is to be complacent in their own destruction. The U.S. is facing an issue. The first high school graduates are showing up as active participants, like the accused Adam Zachary Chesser. Organizations that should know better are being co-opted and corrupted like the Boy Scouts. Muslim Boy Scouts are being indoctrinated in ways of Jihad in Philadelphia. If the group teaches violence and Jihad, its members are valid targets of counterterrorism. Pictures displaying the problem abound.

What is equally frightening is the way security agencies are being told to use a risk-based assessment. It sees children as non-entities, not worthy of being considered terrorist threats. As we move farther and farther from the large scale events of nine eleven, the pressure to drop the guard increases. The push to see all as equal non-entities will include seniors, pregnant women, and disabled children and adults.

If the only way to stop the madness is to target the areas where children are being turned, then the West had better brace for an ugly situation. Otherwise, the battle is lost. The bullet and the IED or bomb does not care how old the puller is. The children, however hateful the task is, must be the target to be stopped.

Elsewhere in Britain, the government says that effective in 2013, it will end the practice of paying multiple social welfare benefits to Muslim immigrants practicing bigamy or polygamy.

A September 2011 British newspaper exposé revealed that tens of thousands of Muslim immigrants in Britain are practicing bigamy or polygamy to collect bigger welfare payments.

Bigamy is a crime in Britain, punishable by up to seven years in prison. But, multicultural policies have fueled a rise in multiple marriages. They grant special rights to Muslim immigrants who want British law to reflect Islamic Sharia law and the welfare system.

The UK recognizes polygamous marriages from countries where they are legal. This applies if both parties were residents of those countries before moving to Britain.

The report shows that Muslim men can take multiple wives, anywhere in the world. They can father any number of children with them. British taxpayers must care for this family.

Muslim immigrants, with a string of wives in separate homes, are claiming benefits for single mothers. This is costing the state tens of millions of pounds.

Those women are eligible for full housing benefits. In some parts of London, that means £106,000 ($250,000) a year. They also get child benefits of £1,000 ($1,500) for a first child, and nearly £700 ($1,000) for each additional child.

The best welfare system exists in societies based on western Christian values. The system is doomed to destruction under abuse by the Islamic philosophies. The system is at risk of collapse when Islamic families use tawriya, taqiyya, and polygamy. The first two Islamic philosophies allow creative lying. They aim to hide that polygamy, a third Islamic practice, is illegal where it is practiced, such as in England. This lets Islamic families collect larger welfare payments than monogamous Christian families living under the law. The welfare system will allow the Muslim faith a higher birth rate because the Muslims are not paying for the full cost of raising their families. Some of this pattern is correlated by the work of Dr. Nicolai Sennels. At the same time, the Islamic families will claim some exemptions. They won't pay for health insurance due to their religion. This will lower their tax bills. The Islamic families will be taking more out collectively then the Islamic families are paying in. There is no similar set up in any Islamic country.

When dealing with a hostile media interview during an election, always give two answers to any question the interviewer asks. The second answer will be the answer to the question asked. The first answer will be the answer to any question the interviewer asked your opponent. If interviewers throw softballs to your opponent, they will ask them to reply to your answer to the same question. So, do your homework to prepare.)

Elected officials must serve the people, not their supporters. Unlike Solyndra, they should use taxpayer dollars to meet taxpayers' needs.

One should not be allowed to vote if one is receiving largesse from the government six months before the election. This does not mean Social Security or retirement checks, but welfare for those not working.

Today people still tip using a one dollar bill as a quick tip. People who are doing that are being cheap and not just with the tip receiver. The people do not take into account inflation. The safe formula is still percents. In today's world for quick tips, use ATM fees as a guide. In short, do not be cheap, it reflects poorly on you.

Get rid of the 1965 Voting Act. Give those states control over their own destiny. Those responsible for the need of the Voting Act are deceased or out of power. It was roughly fifty years ago and time to be a bygone bygone.

If you, as a woman, want a miserable, screaming baby, smoke, use alcohol, drink coffee, or use any other substance that transfers freely between your and the baby's blood systems. This is because the first long term experience the baby will have is drug withdrawals.

More Lawyers = More Government=More Laws=More Regulation=More Taxes and Fines

Remember the largest single organization that has the largest number of lawyers is the government. The government has one product: lawyers. They create regulations, directives, executive orders, and laws that enslave us.

To know if your elected official is worthy of re-election, ask people outside their district. They may be a public joke. Congressman Ocasio-Cortez, Maxine Waters, and Ayanna Soyini Pressley are cases in point. Furthermore, there is always another idiot who will get elected because we did nothing to stop them.

All union officials and all elected or appointed government figures should place their children and grandchildren in public schools for education.

# Death for Apostates, Jail for Blasphemers

**09/13/2022 by Raymond Ibrahim**
**Coptic Solidarity**

**A Libyan court has sentenced a young man to death for "apostasy from Islam."** The Libyan al-Jumhiriyah channel reports that a verdict was issued against a young man, Diya' al-Din Bil'awa. He graduated from the College of Information Technology in 2018.

Diya' was a hafiz, one who had memorized the entire Koran. This suggested he was once an Islamic cleric. So, his apostasy was all the more scandalous.

It is unclear how the accused's apostasy has shown itself. Did he convert to Christianity, as is often the case with Muslim apostates? Or, did he become an outspoken atheist or agnostic?

According to al-Jumhiriyah, sometime in 2019, the accused was "offered" to retract his apostasy and rejoin the fold of Islam, but he refused to do so.

It is clear that the apostasy law cited was in Libya's penal code. It was established after the "Arab Spring" overthrow of Muamar Gaddafi. "We [the U.S.] came, we saw, he died," to quote a then-cackling Secretary of State, Hillary Clinton.

Image of death sentencing for apostasy against Diya' al-Din Bil'awa issued by Libya dated 9/4/2022

This development reminds us of the "Arab Spring." The Western media long portrayed it as a movement to overthrow tyranny and replace it with liberalism. But, like every other Middle Eastern nation, Libya has taken a turn for the worse since then. In 2015, 21 Coptic Christians were beheaded there for their faith.

**In neighboring Egypt, a Cairo appeals court confirmed a five-year prison sentence (with hard labor) for a young Copt, Marco Guirguis Shehata, for "deriding Islam.""** The accusation is based on "evidence" found on his smartphone, which Marco had said was stolen at that time. His father, a modest iron smith, in Kena, north of Luxor, and his entire family were devastated by the unexpectedly harsh sentence.

In just one week, two cases arose. A man was sentenced to death for "apostasy" in Libya. Another was given five years' hard labor for "deriding Islam" in Egypt. They followed the tragic case of "Baby Shenouda." Egyptian authorities took a four-year-old boy from his adoptive Christian parents. They sent him to an orphanage, where he was forcibly "returned" to Islam. Egypt is governed by sharia, which bans adoption. It teaches that every human is a sort of prototypical Muslim at birth. They "lose" their Islam when taught false things or religions. This creates an urgent need to remove this child from loving but Christian parents.

Surely it is high time for the civilized world to acknowledge sharia for what it is—the antithesis of human rights?

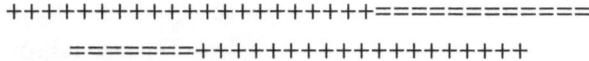

The Tragic Story of 'Baby Shenouda'

09/06/2022 by Raymond Ibrahim

A picture of Shenouda, flanked by his adoptive parents from their recent interview

Another tragic story surrounding a Christian household has just surfaced from Egypt.

**Four years ago, a Coptic priest heard cries emanating from inside his empty church. He located its source, only to discover a newborn baby boy, apparently abandoned by a mother who bore him out of wedlock. The priest entrusted the newborn babe to a childless, pious, couple from his congregation. After 29 years of praying to God for a child, they joyously embraced the boy as their own. They baptized and named him Shenouda, a popular Coptic name, including that of the current pope's predecessor.**

**For the next four years everything went well. The boy—known among the congregation as "Baby Shenouda"—was the pride and joy of his adoptive parents' lives. Seeing him as a miracle-child, a "gift from God," they spared no care or expense on his upbringing. Despite his young age, they taught him the alphabet and several biblical verses, which he memorized in connection with every letter.**

**Then the Egyptian state learned about this otherwise happy development. Egyptian law does not allow for adoption. So, the 4-year-old child was seized from his parents' arms—to cries of "mamma, papa!"—and sent to an orphanage.**

**The police, the ministry of social affairs, and the family-status court decided to seize the child for one reason. Since Shenouda's biological parents' religion is unknown, he must be considered Muslim. This is based on Islamic teaching. Every human is born a kind of prototypical Muslim. They "lose" their Islam only when taught false things or religions, like Christianity.**

At the orphanage, the child was forcibly "returned" to Islam. He got a birth certificate—marked "Muslim" under religion—and an acceptable Muslim name, Yusuf.

Also, Egyptian orphanages are notoriously terrible and overcrowded dungeons. Individual children are "swallowed" by the mass. There, they are often neglected. They fear becoming "street kids" and turning to crime when released.

From the moment when the state seized the child until now, his adoptive parents have been in tears—or, to quote from a recent interview, "living in hell." They have pled with the state to have the child returned. After sobbingly explaining in the interview how her heart "leapt with joy" when she first heard Shenouda say "mamma," his mother even offered to work for free as a servant in the orphanage, just to be near him. The father said he would do "anything"—"shoot me with gunfire even, anything, just so long as I can have my child back!"

All such pleas have fallen on deaf ears. Nor have Egypt's so-called "National Council for Human Rights" or "National Council for Motherhood and Childhood" commented on this.

**A closer look at the intricacies behind the state's decision helps shed light on its "rationale." First, Egyptian family-status law is based on Islamic law. Family-status laws for Christians are based on Christian "laws," but on condition that they do not counter sharia. In this case, adoption is lawful in Christianity. But, it is not applicable since sharia does not allow for adoption. This is based on a well-known precedent of the Prophet Muhammad. To marry Zaynab, the wife of a young man he had adopted, the very concept of adoption had to be nullified. Otherwise, he would have been marrying his daughter-in-law, which is illegal.)**

In other words, the reason Shenouda and his family were targeted is because of their Christian faith. Adoption is illegal in Egypt. But, a family can take an orphan into "custody." The family will care for the child. The child won't inherit or carry the family's name.

But, in this case, the child's background is unknown. He was being raised as a Christian. This has caused the state to act, based on the Islamic teaching cited above. If every human is born a Muslim, obviously it becomes a great "crime" to offer up any orphaned child to a Christian, Jew, or any other non-Muslim parent. This is the primary argument being used by the state against Shenouda's adoptive parents' legal attempts to reclaim the boy.

There is every indication that Shenouda was born to a Christian mother. Or, at least, to a mother who thought Christians would best know how to raise her unwanted child. Otherwise, why abandon the babe in a church?

Yet, the Egyptian state prefers to abandon this 4-year-old boy. They want to avoid raising him as a Christian. Instead, they want him to be a Muslim. So, they throw him into an overcrowded, abusive orphanage. Anything to avoid his being raised by a loving mother and father.

# Islamic Cannibalism

Part A
Cannibalism in the Quran | Quran Explained (wordpress.com)
**Quran Explained**
**From the book of Al-Kortoby; THE COLLECTOR
OF THE QURANIC RULES.**
**January 11, 2010Cannibalism in the Quran**

Posted in Quranic Explanations. Tags: Al-Shafie, Allah, Cannibalism, collectors of the Quranic rules, commentaries, Dead, Eating, Human flesh, Ibn Al-Araby, Imam, Islam, Kortoby, Muslim, Nahed Metwaly, prophet Mohammad, Quran, scholars, swine. Posted by Nahed Metwaly at 8:54 am.

An important and a serious question, "Does Allah of Islam, allow Muslims in the Quran, to eat human flesh?"

The answer is very clearly, "Yes".

Read the following two verses in the Quran,

(1) Quran (2: 173):

"He hath only forbidden you dead meat, and blood, and the flesh of swine, and that on which any other name hath been invoked besides that of Allah. But if one is forced by necessity, without wilful disobedience, nor transgressing due limits,- then is he guiltless. For Allah is Oft-forgiving Most Merciful" (Surah The Cow 2:173).

(2) Quran (16: 115):

"He has only forbidden you dead meat, and blood, and the flesh of swine, and any (food) over which the name of other than Allah has been invoked. "But if one must, without disobedience or transgression, then Allah is Oft-Forgiving, Most Merciful." (Surah The Bee 16:115).

The reference of the commentaries on these verses is: The book of "Al-Kortoby", the collector of the Quranic rules.

Volume 1 of the 3rd edition introduces this book. It is by Imam Shams El-Din Abi Abdallah Mohamed Bin Ahmad Ben Abi Bakr Farag Al-Ansari Al-Kortoby, who died in 671 AH. It is published by Dar El-Ghad El-Araby, 3 Danesh Street, Abassia, Cairo, Egypt, Telephone (2-824-329).

He said in page 3,

"In the name of Allah, the merciful and compassionate. This book is published under the supervision of the scholars of Al-Azhar, the world's largest Islamic university." All publishing rights are reserved to Dar El-Ghad El-Araby, Cairo".

He continues,

"This edition is corrected and certified by the "Council of Islamic Research of Al-Azhar." They published it on 9 November 1988, 29 Rabie I of the Islamic year 1409."

In page 716 in volume 1, Al-Kortoby gives these comments,

"If someone is in dire need and finds a dead animal, he may eat it because it is 'Halal' (lawful). But, he must not eat a swine or human." There is a light prevention and a strong prevention. These are the rules. One hates to have sex with his sister. But, it is lawful to have sex with a foreigner. This is the condition for theses rules. Eating the flesh of a human is not allowed.

Yet, the scholars Ahmad and Dawoud protested. They said that prophet Mohammad said, "Breaking the bones of a dead body is like breaking the bones of a live body." Al-Shafie said, "One may eat the flesh of a human body. It is not allowed to kill a Muslim or a free non-Muslim under Muslim rule. The latter is useful to society. Nor may one kill a prisoner, as he belongs to other Muslims. But you may kill an enemy fighter or an adulterer and eat his body".

Dawoud slandered Al-Mozny by addressing Al-Mozny saying, "You allowed eating the flesh of the prophets". Ibn Sharie responded also to Al-Mozny by saying, "You allowed killing the prophets and did not allow eating the flesh of the infidels".

Ibn Al-Araby said, "I should not eat human flesh unless it saves a starving person. Allah knows best."

Dear reader,

I reported to you what is written in the commentaries of Al-Kortoby. I wrote exactly what I found without changing a word. But let me put an extra light on these commentaries. Al-Kortoby mentioned two kinds of preventions, a light one and a strong one and he left the reader to chose between the two. He gave the example of having a sexual relation with a sister or with a foreigner. He prefers the light prevention and not the strong one and left the reader to chose between the two.

But Imam El-Shefie was more clear and he courageously said, "Human flesh may be eaten". He added, "An enemy fighter or an adulterer may be killed and his flesh be eaten". More seriously, Dawoud protested against Al-Muzni. He said, "If you allowed the eating of the flesh of the prophets (sarcastically, I say, 'for fear they would not be slaughtered in the Islamic way'), you should also allow eating the flesh of the infidels." The final verdict for him, "Human flesh should not be eaten unless that would safe the life of the eater from starving to death and Allah knows best".

Here is a great danger to the whole world. Islam, the Quran, and the scholars of Islam allow the Muslim to eat the flesh of the non-Muslim if that saves the Muslim from starving to death. We all know about the economic crisis which haunts the whole world these days. As we said, Imam El-Shafie said it very clearly, "An enemy fighter or an adulterer may be killed and his flesh may be eaten". And in the eyes of every Muslim, a non-Muslim is an enemy fighter and an adulterer.

I challenge any person who denies what I said, as by the grace of God, I have all the references which I got this information from.

This subject is to be continued.

Nahed

Part B
https://shoebat.com/2016/08/29/isis-cannibals-take-250-children-under-the-age-of-four-throws-them-into-dough-kneader-ovens-and-meat-grinders-forces-the-mother-of-one-two-year-old-to-eat-her-sons-ground-up-body/

ISIS cannibals took 250 children under four. They threw them into dough kneaders, ovens, and meat grinders. They forced the mother of a two-year-old to eat her son's ground-up body.

by Andrew Bieszad on August 29, 2016 in Featured

Arabs-waving-entrails-of-butchered-Israelis-in-Ramallah

Muslims holding and eating human entrails

We have documented on Shoebat.com cannibalism among Muslims. Islam permits and encourages it, especially against non-Muslims. From an Islamic perspective, the logic is simple- non-Muslims are not human, and therefore as they are not human, it may be possible to eat them.

An ISIS soldier dissecting and eating a human heart

We have documented the human butcheries the Muslims operated in Serbia during the 1994 war. Cannibalism among ISIS is so rampant that it has caused very rare diseases to reappear. Those diseases are caused only by cannibalism. This story, however, is a new low. It shows Muslims butchering children with food processors and feeding the dead kids to their parents.

**In a Commons debate on the Islamic State's genocide, two MPs recounted a Yazidi girl's testimony. She was kidnapped and raped. Her father and brother were killed before her eyes. She witnessed a 9-year-old girl being raped to death. A 2-year-old boy was killed, ground into meat, and then "fed to his mother who did not know what she was eating."''**

The Yazidi girl, "Ekhlas," spoke with MPs on April 19, 2016. She said, "The Daesh killed the men and they took the girls. Any girls over nine were raped." MP Natalie McGarry (Glasgow) repeated this in her speech in the Commons. McGarry said she wrote down Ekhlas's testimony, "took down her words directly." "She spoke of Christians being killed and tortured, and of children being beheaded in front of their parents," recounted MP Bruce. "She showed us recent footage of herself talking with mothers—more than one—who had seen their children crucified." "Another woman had seen 250 children put through a dough kneader and burnt in an oven," said Bruce. "The oldest was four years old." (source)

Remember, every idiot who is in favor of mass Muslim immigration is promoting this whether he realizes it or not.

# Exposed: Decade-Old Plan to Create Islamic State—and Obama Helped

By Raymond Ibrahim on November 6, 2014in
Islam, Other Matters FrontPage Magazine

The birth of the Islamic state and the caliphate are often seen as 2014's "big shockers." But, an al-Qaeda insider predicted them in detail and on time nearly a decade ago.

On August 12, 2005, Spiegel Online International published "The Future of Terrorism: What al-Qaeda Really Wants." It was a review of a book by Fouad Hussein, a Jordanian journalist with close access to al-Qaeda. The article was by Yassin Musharbash. It noted that Abu Musab al-Zarqawi, who pioneered the beheading videos, sought to "strike terror into the hearts" of infidels (Koran 3:151).

Hussein's book, Al Zarqawi: Al Qaeda's Second Generation, states: "I interviewed a range of al-Qaeda members with different ideologies to see how the war between the terrorists and Washington would develop."

The book details al-Qaeda's master plan. Its "second generation," the "Islamic State," follows much of Zarqawi's way of doing things. It aims to resurrect a caliphate. This plan is so outlandish that Yassin Musharbash, author of a Spiegel article reviewing Hussein's book, doubts it can work. Thus, al-Qaeda's plan proves their blind, brutal single-mindedness. There is "no way" they can follow it "step by step." The idea they could set up a caliphate in the entire Islamic world is absurd. The following "scenario should be judged skeptically.'"

Yet it is all the more remarkable that much of this plan—especially those phases dismissed as infeasible by Musharbash (four and five)—have come to pass.

I will reproduce the seven phases of al-Qaeda's master plan. They are in Musharbash's nearly ten-year-old article (in bullet points and italics, bold for emphasis). My comments are interspersed for context. Phases four and five are important. They detail recent goals, most of which have been achieved as planned.

An Islamic Caliphate in Seven Easy Steps

•The First Phase, known as "the awakening," has already been done. It was supposed to last from 2000 to 2003. More precisely, it was to run from the September 11, 2001, terrorist attacks in New York and Washington to the fall of Baghdad in 2003. The aim of the attacks of 9/11 was to provoke the US into declaring war on the Islamic world and thereby "awakening" Muslims. "The first phase was judged by the strategists and masterminds behind al-Qaeda as very successful," writes Hussein. "The battle field was opened up and the Americans and their allies became a closer and easier target." The terrorist network is also reported as being satisfied that its message can now be heard "everywhere."

Much of this is accurate and makes sense. Sadly, if any eyes were opened after the 9/11 attacks, they weren't Western ones. Certainly, they weren't those of Western leaders, the media, or academics. But, to many Muslims, the 9/11 strikes were inspiring. They believed Osama bin Laden's claim that America is a "paper tiger." A few years after the 9/11 attacks, Americans elected a man with a Muslim name and heritage for president. This was despite his actions, including banning knowledge of Islam. They empowered the same ideology behind the attacks. Meanwhile, the average Muslim relearned their religion's truths. The "infidel" is an existential enemy. Jihad against him is a duty, as al-Qaeda and others had shown.

•**The Second Phase** "Opening Eyes" is, according to Hussein's definition, the period we are now in [writing in 2005] and should last until 2006. Hussein says the terrorists hope to make the western conspiracy aware of the "Islamic community." Hussein believes this is a phase in which al-Qaeda wants an organization to develop into a movement. The network is banking on recruiting young men during this period. Iraq should become the center for all global operations, with an "army" set up there and bases established in other Arabic states.

This too is accurate. During this time, the "Islamic community," the umma, became more visible. There were attacks and riots after any perceived "insult" to Islam. This led to demands for appeasement and accusations of "Islamophobia." If there weren't any spectacular terror attacks like 9/11, young Muslim men were quietly enlisting and training in the jihad, or "radicalizing," as the West calls it." Al-Qaeda went from being an "organization" to a "movement"—international "radicalization." Most importantly, Iraq, as the world now knows, certainly did become the "center for all global operations" with an "army" of jihadis set up there.

•**The Third Phase** This is described as "Arising and Standing Up" and should last from 2007 to 2010. "There will be a focus on Syria," prophesies Hussein, based on what his sources told him. The fighting cadres are supposedly already prepared and some are in Iraq. Attacks on Turkey and—even more explosive— in Israel are predicted. Al-Qaeda's leaders hope attacks on Israel will gain it recognition. The author also believes that countries neighboring Iraq, such as Jordan, are also in danger.

Much of this third phase as described and transpired seems to have been an extension of phase two. In retrospect, there certainly appears to have been a focus on Syria, even if the jihad started there one year behind schedule (2011). And many of the jihadis were "already prepared" and "some are in Iraq." None of this was a surprise, of course, as U.S. intelligence always indicated that if American forces withdrew from Iraq, the jihadis would take over.

•**The Fourth Phase** Between 2010 and 2013, Hussein writes that al-Qaeda will aim to bring about the collapse of the hated Arabic governments. The estimate is that "the creeping loss of the regimes' power will lead to a steady growth in strength within al-Qaeda." At the same time attacks will be carried out against oil suppliers and the US economy will be targeted using cyber terrorism.

This is immensely prophetic. The timeline (2010-2013) coincides with the "Arab Spring." It ended with Islamic terrorists taking over several Arab countries once ruled by secular autocrats. These include Egypt (the Muslim Brotherhood, which is al-Qaeda's "Dr. Jekyll"), Libya (al-Qaeda/Islamic jihadis), and Syria (al-Qaeda/Islamic jihadis and the Islamic State, al-Qaeda's "second generation"). The Obama administration played a major role in empowering the jihadis in these nations in the name of "democracy.""

•**The Fifth Phase** This will be the point at which an Islamic state, or caliphate, can be declared. The plan is that, by 2016, Western influence in the Islamic world will be weak. Israel will be much weakened, too. Then, there will be no fear of resistance. Al-Qaeda hopes that by then the Islamic state will be able to bring about a new world order.

Again, right on time: In 2014, the "Islamic State" declared a "caliphate." Many Muslims worldwide pledged their allegiance, if not their slaughter. Inspired "lone wolves" began beheading "infidels" in the West. The administration, in the name of "democracy," empowered jihadis during the "Arab Spring" in Egypt, Libya, and Syria. It also helped create the Islamic State. It did this by withdrawing U.S. forces that were keeping al-Qaeda at bay in Iraq. In 2007, George W. Bush said, "Withdrawing [military forces] before our commanders say we are ready would be dangerous for Iraq, the region, and the U.S." It would mean surrendering Iraq's future to Al Qaeda. It would mean that we'd be risking mass killings on a horrific scale. It would mean we allow the terrorists to establish a safe haven in Iraq to replace the one they lost in Afghanistan. It would increase the chance that U.S. troops would have to return to confront a more dangerous enemy." All of these predictions have proven remarkably prescient. Not because Bush was a prophet, but because U.S. intelligence understood the situation in Iraq. It briefed Obama on it, just as it did Bush. In 2011, Obama declared the Iraq war a success and pulled out U.S. troops. This left the way open for jihadists to resurrect the caliphate.

•**The Sixth Phase** Hussein believes that from 2016 onwards there will a period of "total confrontation." Once the caliphate is declared, the "Islamic army" will spark the "fight between the believers and the non-believers." Osama bin Laden often predicted this.

This needs clarification. Many assume the "fight between the believers and the non-believers" is between Muslims and non-Muslims. This is not always the case. Soon after the caliphate was announced, the Islamic State declared a jihad on "apostates" and "hypocrites." This meant all "apostate" or "infidel" Arab leaders, like Bashar al-Assad, and Muslims deemed not "Islamic" enough." The new caliph chose the name "Abu Bakr." It was the name of the first historic caliph (632-634). His caliphate was marked by fighting to bring back into Islam the Arabs who had broken away after Muhammad's death. Afterwards, all the Arab tribes united under Islam. Then, the great historic conquests, or jihads, against neighboring "infidels," took place.

•**The Seventh Phase** This final stage is described as "definitive victory." Hussein writes that the terrorists believe their caliphate will succeed. The world's people will be beaten down by "one-and-a-half billion Muslims." This phase should be completed by 2020, although the war shouldn't last longer than two years.

Phase seven remains to be seen, as it is has another five years to go. Actor Ben Affleck recently echoed this view. He kept apologizing for Islam, saying, "There are a billion and a half Muslims." At any rate, the preceding phases have all largely come to pass. The West did nothing to prevent them, and sometimes even aided them. So, there is no good reason to think Western leaders will stop the final phase. A unified, aggressive, expansionist, and possibly nuclear-armed caliphate is preparing to terrorize its neighbors on a grand scale—just like its historic predecessor did for centuries.

# Obama The Great Deceiver

On June 28, 2006, President Obama said in prepared remarks: Given America's growing diversity, sectarianism poses a greater danger than ever. We are no longer just a Christian nation. We are also a Jewish, Muslim, Buddhist, Hindu, and nonbelieving nation. This assertion is a lie.

This country was founded as and is a Judeo – Christian nation. The Constitution's backbone is the Ninth Commandment, Exodus 20:16: "You shall not bear false witness against your neighbor." The Constitution's strength rests on that principle. If one will lie after taking the Oath of Congress, one will lie everywhere else. Congressional hearings have proven this. They were conducted by Senators, Congresswomen, Congressmen, and various executive branch members, including President Biden. Congress has repeatedly proven that Congress is not willing to keep the Congress free of lies and deception.

There was no Hindu, no Buddhist, and no Moslem in the Founding of the Constitution. This is especially true because there was no tolerance of the Sanctified Lies as Islam allows with Kitman, Maruna, Tawriya or Taqiyya. Remember the first great battles the United States Navy had after the War of Independence was with the Barbary Coast Pirates.

It is true the U.S. now has Hindus, Buddhists, and Muslims. But, it was founded on Judeo-Christian principles, which the Constitution reflects. Muslims still support and have 700,000 slaves in parts of Africa and the Middle East, including children and women. Where ever Islam goes, Slavery will follow.

Now to the question, what is the first lie in Congress? Ask any Islamic follower. The lie is the Oath of office, to wit: "I do solemnly swear (or affirm) that I will support and defend the Constitution of the United States against all enemies, foreign and domestic; that I will bear true faith and allegiance to the same. This is the first lie for any Muslim in Congress or as President. Muslims are charged with spreading Sharia worldwide. There are no Women's Rights. But, there is Slavery, Lying, and Might makes Right for starters. Children are property. There is stoning for Adultery and limb amputation for theft and lying.

That is what will happen when Judeo-Christian roots of the Constitution are removed destroying a government of, by, and for the people.

This is the world Obama wants with a return to Islamic Slavery.

How to wipe out Islamic terror: Dr. Subramanian Swamy-India

Posted on July 29, 2011by janamejayan

The 'minority' commission is using secular law to limit Indian citizens' rights. They want to express their fears of terrorist attacks by Islamic groups bent on destroying Hindustan. We are republishing Dr.Subramanian Swamy's article so you can judge it yourself. The saying is true that if one is not pro-Indian then he is anti-Indian. If one is not pro-Hindu then he is anti-Hindu. Most secularists fall in this category.

Janamejayan

# How to wipe out Islamic terror: Dr. Subramaniam Swamy

The terrorist blast in Mumbai on July 13, 2011 requires a decisive soul searching by Hindus of India. Hindus cannot accept being killed in this Halal fashion. It means, to bleed to death, every day, until the nation collapses.

Terrorism, I define here as the illegal use of force to overawe the civilian population to make it do or not do an act against their will and well-being.

There are about 40 reported and unreported terrorist attacks per month in the country. That is why the recent US National Counter-Terrorism Centre publication A Chronology of International Terrorism states: 'India suffered more terrorist acts than any other country'.

While the PM thinks that Maoists' threat is most serious, I think Islamic terrorism is an even more serious existential threat. Without today's Union Home Minister, PM, and UPA chairperson, we could eliminate the Maoists in a month. I did it with the LTTE in Tamil Nadu as a senior minister in 1991. MGR did it with the Naxalites in the early 1980s. Islamic threat to the nation is different.

Why is Islamic terrorism our number one problem of national security? About this there will be no doubt in anyone's mind after 2012. By that year, I expect a Taliban takeover in Pakistan and the Americans to flee Afghanistan. Then, Islam will confront Hinduism to 'complete unfinished business'. The new Al Qaeda leader, who succeeded Osama Bin Laden, has declared that India is the group's top target, not the USA.

Fanatic Muslims consider Hindu dominated India as "an unfinished chapter of Islamic conquests". I may be recalled that all other countries conquered by Islam became 100% converted to Islam within two decades of the Islamic invasion. India is the exception. Undivided India in 1947 was 75% Hindu even after 800 years of brutal Islamic rule. That is jarring for the Islamic fanatics.

Since 1947, all Hindu-Muslim riots in India were ignited by Muslim fanatics, according to the Commissions of Inquiry set up after each riot. Even the Gujarat riots were triggered by the brutal killing of 56 women and children by setting fire to a rail coach in Godhra.

By today's definition these riots are all terroristacts. Muslims, though a minority in India, still have fanatics who dare tolead violent attacks against Hindus. Other Muslims of India just lump it, sulk or rejoice. That is the history from Babar's time to Aurangzeb. There have been exceptions to this apathy of Muslims. In the old days, there was Dara Shikoh. Today, there are M J Akbar and Salman Haidar. They are not afraid to speak out against Islamic terror. But, they remain exceptions.

Blame the Hindus

In one sense, I do not blame the Muslim fanatics for targeting Hindus. I blame us Hindus who have taken their individuality permitted in Sanatana Dharma to the extreme. Millions of Hindus can self-organise and hold the Kumbh Mela without state help. But, they all leave for home, unaware of the targeting of Hindus in Kashmir, Mau, Melvisharam, and Malappuram. They do nothing to help organise Hindus. If half the Hindus vote together, a Hindu party will have a two-thirds majority in Parliament and Assemblies.

Secularists now cite Hindu fanatics' terrorist attacks on Muslims and other minorities. But these attacks are mostly state sponsored, often by the Congress itself, and not by Hindu 'non-state actors'. Muslim-led attacks are all by 'non-state actors' except for the ISI and rogue elements in Pakistan's army aiding them, as state sponsoring.

Fanatic Muslims have attacked to demoralise Hindus. They aim to make Hindus yield what they should not. The goal is to undermine and dismantle India's Hindu foundation. This is the unfinished war of 1,000 years which Osama bin Laden talks about. The first terror tactics in India were used in Bengal in 1946. Suhrawardy and Jinnah used them to terrorize Hindus into accepting the demand for Pakistan. The Congress party claiming to represent the Hindus capitulated, and handed 25 per cent of India on a platter to Mohammed Ali Jinnah. Now they want the remaining 75 per cent.

Forces against Hindus

This is not to say that other stooges have not targeted Hindus. Since Independence, a British-inspired Dravidian movement, led by E V Ramaswamy Naicker, tried to debunk Hinduism in the name of rationalism. It also terrorized the Brahmins, the priestly class, for promoting it.

The movement's organisation, the Dravida Kazhagam (DK), had venerated Ravana for 50 years to spite the Hindu adoration of Rama. They sought to vulgarise the abduction of Sita. The DK then learnt, too late, that Ravana was a Brahmin and a pious bhakta of Lord Shiva. The DK, after defaming the Ramayana, have now become stooges of the anti-Indian LTTE. The LTTE specializes in killing Sri Lanka's Hindu Tamil leaders. Of course the DK has now been orphaned by the decimation of the LTTE.

Civil war situation

In the 1960s, the Christian missionaries had inspired the Nagas. The Nagas also wanted to further amputate Bharat Mata by seeking secession of Nagaland from the nation. In the 1980s, the Hindus of Manipur were targeted by foreign-trained elements. Manipuris were told:give up Hinduism or be killed. Since the 1990s, militants allied with Pakistan-trained terrorists in Kashmir have targeted Hindus. They drove out the Hindu Pandits or killed them and dishonored their women.

The targeting of Hindus is widely perceived. Muslims in India are mostly passive spectators. So, the foreign backers of Islamic terrorists are starting to engage in terrorist acts. These could spark a nationwide conflict between Muslims and Hindus, like in Serbia and Bosnia.

We cannot divide Muslims into 'moderates' and 'extremists.' 'Moderates' just capitulate when confronted. Recently, Pakistan's civilian government banned 'kite flying.' The Taliban considers it 'Hindu.' Moderate governments of Malaysia and Kazhakstan are now demolishing Hindu temples.

Collective response

The first lesson from recent history is this: Islamic terrorists in India target Hindus. A slow process is radicalizing some Indian Muslims, leading them to commit suicide attacks against Hindus. It is to undermine the Hindu psyche and create fear of civil war that terror attacks are organised.

Hindus are the target. So, they must unite against the terrorist. They should not feel isolated or complacent because they are not personally affected. If one Hindu dies merely because he or she was a Hindu, then a bit of every Hindu also dies. This is an essential mental attitude. It is a part of a virat Hindu. For a fuller discussion of virat Hindu, see my book, Hindus Under Siege: The Way Out (Haranand, 2006).

Therefore, we need today a collective mindset as Hindus to stand against the Islamic terrorist. In this response, Muslims of India can join us if they genuinely feel for the Hindu. That they do, I will not believe, unless they acknowledge with pride that though they may be Muslims, their ancestors are Hindus.

They find it hard to accept their ancestry. The Muslim mullah would reject it. It would weaken their faith and tempt them to convert back to Hinduism. These religious leaders preach hatred and violence against the kafir, i.e., the Hindus (see Quran, Chapter 8, verse 12). They do this to keep their followers' faith. The Islamic terrorist outfits, e.g the SIMI, has already resolved that India is Darul Harab, and they are committed to make it Darul Islam. That makes them free of any moral compunction whatsoever in dealing with Hindus.

Brihad Hindu Samaj

But still, if any Muslim does so acknowledge his or her Hindu legacy, then we Hindus can accept him or her as a part of the Brihad Hindu Samaj, which is Hindustan. India that is Bharat that is Hindustan is a nation of Hindus and others whose ancestors are Hindus. Even Parsis and Jews in India have Hindu ancestors. Some, who refuse to acknowledge this, can't stay. Also, foreigners who become Indian citizens by registration can stay, but they can't vote or be elected.

Hence, to begin with, any policy to combat terrorism must begin with requiring each and every Hindu becoming a committed or virat Hindu. To be a virat Hindu, one must have a Hindu mindset. This mindset recognizes two things: vyaktigat charitra and rashtriya charitra. They are, respectively, personal and national character.

It is not enough if one is pious, honest and educated. That is the personal character only. National character is a mindset actively and vigorously committed to the sanctity and integrity of the nation. For example, our prime minister, Manmohan Singh, has high personal character (vyaktigat charitra). But, by being a rubber stamp of a semi-literate Sonia Gandhi and waffling on all national issues, he has proved that he has no rashtriya charitra.

The second lesson for combating today's terrorism is: all terrorists in India aim to destroy the Hindu civilization by demoralising and undermining Hindus. So, we must never capitulate or concede to their demands. The basic policy has to be: never yield to any demand of the terrorists. That necessary resolve has not been shown in our recent history. Instead ever since we conceded Pakistan in 1947 under duress, we have been mostly yielding time and again.

Bowing to terrorists

In 1989, to free Mufti Mohammed Sayeed's daughter, Rubaiyya, the V P Singh government released five terrorists from Indian jails. Terrorists had kidnapped her. This made these criminals heroes to Kashmiri separatists and fence sitters. They had brought India's Hindu establishment to its knees. To save Rubaiyya it was not necessary to surrender to terrorist demands.

A worse capitulation to terrorists in our modern history was in the Indian Airlines IC-814 hijack in December 1999 staged in Kandahar. The government released three terrorists without court permission. It was required since they were in judicial custody. Also, they were royal guests. A senior minister escorted them on the PM's special Boeing to Kandahar, instead of being shoved across the Indo-Pakistan border.

Worse still, all three, after being freed, went back to Pakistan. They then created three terrorist groups to kill Hindus. Mohammed Azhar, "a mere harmless cleric," per National Security Advisor Brijesh Mishra, led the LeT to savage, repeated attacks on Hindus across India, from Bangalore to Srinagar, after his release. Since mid-2000, Azhar is responsible for the killing of over 2,000 Hindus and the attack on Parliament on December 13, 2001. Omar Sheikh, who helped al-Qaeda, is in US custody for killing journalist Daniel Pearl. The third, Zargar, is now killing Hindus in Doda and Jammu after founding Al-Mujahideen Jingaan.

This Kandahar episode proves that we should never negotiate with terrorists, never yield. If you do, then sooner or later you will end up losing more lives than you will ever save by a deal with terrorists.

Moment of truth

The third lesson is that, no matter how small, the nation must retaliate for any terrorist incident. It must respond with massive retaliation, not measured, 'sober' responses. Otherwise what is the alternative? Walk meekly to death expecting that our 'sober' responses will be rewarded by our neighbours and their patrons? We will be back to 1100 AD fooled into suicidal credulity. We should not be ghouls for punishment from terrorists and their patrons. We should retaliate.

For example, a planned attack on the Ayodhya temple was not a big terrorist incident. But, we should have massively retaliated by re-building the Ram temple at the site.

This is Kaliyug, and hence there is no room for sattvic responses to evil people. Hindu religion has a concept of apat dharma and we should invoke it. This is the moment of truth for us. We must organize to survive as a civilization. Or, we will vanish like the Persians, Babylonians, and Egyptians did centuries ago before the brutal Islamic onslaught. For that our motto should be Saam, Dhaam, Bheda, Danda.

Poverty is no factor

What motivates the Islamic terrorists in India? Many advise us Hindus to tackle the root cause of terrorism. They say to avoid retaliating against terrorists. And pray what is the root cause'?

Bleeding heart liberals say that terrorists are a product of illiteracy, poverty, oppression, and discrimination. They argue that instead of eliminating them, the root cause of these four disabilities in society should be removed. Only then terrorism will disappear. Before replying, I must say I doubt these liberals. Or, more accurately, I doubt these promiscuous intellectuals. They seek to deaden the emotive power of the individual and render him passive (inculcate 'majboori' in our psyche). A nation state cannot survive for long with such a capitulationist mentality.

It is rubbish to say that terrorists who mastermind the attacks are poor. Osama bin laden for example is a billionaire. Islamic terrorists are patronised by those states that have grown rich from oil revenues. In Britain, the terrorists arrested so far for the bombings are all well-to-do persons. Nor are terrorists uneducated. Most of terrorist leaders are doctors, chartered accountants, MBAs and teachers. For example, in the failed Times Square New York episode, the Islamic terrorist Shahzad studied and got an MBA from a reputed US university. He was from a highly placed family in Pakistan. He certainly faced no discrimination and oppression in his own country. The nine who hijacked four planes on September 11, 2001, and flew them into the World Trade Towers in New York and other targets, were not oppressed in the U.S. So, it is rubbish to say that poverty causes terrorism.

If we accept the Left-wing liberals' argument, does it mean that, in Islamic countries, the oppressed non-Islamic minorities can resort to terrorism? In the Valley, where Muslims are the majority, Article 370 of the Constitution gives them privileges. But, the minority Hindus have been slaughtered, raped, and dispossessed. They have become refugees in squalid conditions in their own country.

It is also a ridiculous idea that terrorists cannot be deterred because they are irrational, willing to die, and have no 'return address'. Terrorist masterminds have political goals and a method in their madness. A way to deter terrorism is to defeat its political goals. We must also discredit them with counter-terrorist action. How is that strategy to be structured? This year, Robert Trager and Dessislava Zagorcheva published a brilliant paper. It is titled "Deterring Terrorism." It appears in International Security, vol 30, No 3, Winter 2005/06, pp 87-123. It provides the general principles to structure a strategy to deter terrorism.

Goal-strategy

Using these principles, I propose a strategy to counter Islamic terrorism in India. It is to negate its political goals, if the Muslim community fails to condemn them as un-Islamic.

Goal 1: Overawe India on Kashmir.

Strategy: Remove Article 370, and re-settle ex-servicemen in the Valley. Create Panun Kashmir for Hindu Pandit community. Look or create opportunity to take over PoK. If Pakistan continues to back terrorists, assist the Baluchis and Sindhis to struggle for independence.

Goal 2: Blast our temples and kill Hindu devotees.

Strategy: Remove the masjid in Kashi Vishwanath temple complex, and 300 others in other sites as a tit-for-tat.

Goal 3: Make India into Darul Islam.

Strategy: Implement a Uniform Civil Code. Make Sanskrit learning and singing of Vande Mataram compulsory. Declare India a Hindu Rashtra. Only non-Hindus who proudly acknowledge their Hindu ancestry can vote. Re-name India as Hindustan as a nation of Hindus and those whose ancestors are Hindus.

Goal 4: Change India's demography by illegal immigration, conversion, and refusal to adopt family planning.

Strategy: Enact a national law prohibiting conversion from Hindu religion to any other religion. Re-conversion will not be banned. Declare caste is not birth-based but code of discipline based. Welcome non-Hindus to re-convert to the caste of their choice provided they adhere to the code of discipline. Annex land from Bangladesh in proportion to the illegal migrants from that country staying in India. At present, northern one-third from Sylhet to Khulna can be annexed to re-settle the illegal migrants.

Goal 5: Denigrate Hinduism through vulgar writings and mosque, madrassa, and church sermons. This will cause Hindus to lose self-respect and be ready to capitulate.

Strategy: Spread a Hindu mindset (see my book, Hindutva and National Renaissance, Haranand, 2010).

India can solve its terrorist problem in five years with a deterrent strategy. But, we must learn the four lessons above. We need a Hindu mindset to make bold, risky, and hard decisions to defend the nation. If the Jews can change from meek lambs to fiery lions in just 10 years, it is not hard for Hindus, who are 83% of India, to do so in five years.

Guru Gobind Singh has shown us the way already, how just five fearless persons under spiritual guidance can transform a society. If half the Hindu voters vote as Hindus for a party committed to a Hindu agenda, we can create a tool for change. And that ultimately is the bottom line in the strategy to deter terrorism in a democratic Hindustan at this moment of truth.

Note: One other aspect that is not noted is to give every Muslim Suicide Bomber a sex change operation and bury them with a piece of a swine in their body. That way they are always unclean according to Islamic beliefs. You have to fight the terrorist using the terrorist beliefs.

**(Note: To stop Islamic terrorism, announce and follow through: Anyone convicted of terrorism, or killed as a terrorist, will get a mandatory sex change. This includes dead bodies.)**

# Boris Johnson said that Islamophobia is a 'natural reaction' to Islam and that 'Islam is the problem'

*Adam Bienkov Nov 27, 2019, 5:02 AM*

Muslim leaders accuse Boris Johnson's Conservative party of allowing Islamophobia to "fester" in the UK.

*"It is abundantly clear to many Muslims that the Conservative Party tolerate Islamophobia," the group said.*

*Johnson has previously claimed that Islamophobia is a "natural reaction" to Islam.*

*He wrote in the Spectator in 2005 that "the problem is Islam. Islam is the problem."*

*The prime minister also compared Muslim women to "letterboxes" and bank robbers.*

*Johnson has dropped a previous pledge to hold an inquiry into Islamophobia within the Conservative party.*

*Visit Business Insider's homepage for more stories.*

*Boris Johnson's Conservative party has been accused by Muslim leaders in the UK of allowing Islamophobia to "fester" within their ranks.*

"The Conservative Party has a severe issue with Islamophobia," the group said in a statement on Tuesday. "They have denied, dismissed, and deceived about it."

*They added: "Many Muslims see that the Conservative Party tolerates Islamophobia. It allows it to fester in society and fails to root it out.""*

Business Insider examined the prime minister's record. It shows he has sought to downplay and justify Islamophobia in the UK.

*Islamophobia is 'a natural reaction'*

*In 2005, Johnson wrote in the Spectator that he believed it was only "natural" for the public to be scared of Islam.*

"To any non-Muslim reader of the Koran, Islamophobia — fear of Islam — seems a natural reaction. That text is meant to provoke it," he wrote.

*"Judged only on its scripture, it is the most sectarian of all religions. Its mosques preach a heartless view of unbelievers.""*

*'Islam is the problem'*

*Boris Johnson Oli Scarff/Getty Images*

*After the London bombings, he questioned the loyalty of British Muslims. He insisted that the country must accept that "Islam is the problem.""*

"It will take great courage and skill to win over the many thousands of British Muslims. They are alienated. We must show them that their faith must align with British values and loyalty to Britain," he wrote.

*"That means disposing of the first taboo, and accepting that the problem is Islam. Islam is the problem."*

*He added: "What is going on in these mosques and madrasas? When is someone going to get 18th century on Islam's medieval ass?" Comparing Muslim women who wear the burqa to 'letterboxes'*

Last year, Boris Johnson was reported to the Equalities Commission. He compared Muslim women in burqas to "letter boxes" and bank robbers.

The former foreign secretary wrote in a Telegraph article that "it's ridiculous that people should choose to look like letter boxes." He added that any female student who looked "like a bank robber" at school or in a lecture should be asked to remove it.

Johnson has repeatedly refused to apologize for the comments. He said earlier this month that the article was a "liberal" argument against banning the burqa.

*Islamophobia goes 'right up to the top' of the Conservative party.*

*Baroness Warsi Getty*

*Former Conservative co-chair Baroness Warsi told Business Insider last year that Islamophobia goes "right up to the top" of the Conservative party.*

*"It's very widespread [in the Conservative party]. It exists right from the grassroots, all the way up to the top," she told BI.*

She said that Islamophobia was now "very widespread" in the party. It was being ignored at the highest levels for electoral reasons.

However, Johnson has dropped a prior pledge. He will only hold a broader inquiry into all types of prejudice in society.

*Our Brexit Insider Facebook group is the best source for news and analysis on Britain's EU exit. It comes from Business Insider's political reporters. Join here.*

*SEE ALSO: The Islamophobia scandal in the Conservative party goes 'right up to the top'*

# What is happening in your neighborhood that you do not know?

## Part A

Terror threatened Germany plans to put 14-YEAR-OLD jihadis under surveillance

GERMAN MPs will vote tomorrow on plans to lower the age for monitoring suspected jihadis. This shows that the liberal European powerhouse is getting tough on terror.

By TOM BATCHELOR 12:00, Thu, Jun 23, 2016 | UPDATED: 12:24, Thu, Jun 23, 2016

German police on an anti-terror mission

If approved, the state's domestic intelligence agency can track and collect data on suspected radicalized teens as young as 14, down from 16.

Germany has faced a wave of terror attacks by teenage fanatics. This includes an April attack on a Sikh temple in Essen by two 16-year-olds linked to the radical Salafist community.

## AND IN THE UNITED STATES
FBI, Philly DA's office announces arrest in terrorism probe

The 17-year-old male was arrested Friday on state charges and was allegedly communicating with the group KTJ.

By6abc digital staffUpdated Aug. 14, 2023 3:27 pm

Jacqueline Maguire speaking at a podium

FBI Special Agent in Charge of the Philadelphia Field Office Jacqueline Maguire announcing an arrest in the terrorism case on August 14, 2023. (Tom MacDonald/WHYY)

This story originally appeared on 6abc.

A 17-year-old teenager in Philadelphia has been arrested in connection with a terrorism probe.

At a press conference on Monday, FBI Special Agent Jacqueline Maguire said a 17-year-old male was arrested Friday on state charges. He allegedly communicated with the group Katibat al Tawhid wal Jihad (KTJ).

KTJ was designated as a global terrorist group in 2022 and is affiliated with al-Qaeda, officials said.

The teen suspect allegedly sent and received terrorist propaganda. He also tried to go abroad to join or support the terrorist group.

Maguire said the teen had access to guns. He had also bought items used to make bombs.

"He bought tactical equipment, wiring, chemicals, and remote detonators," said Maguire.

The teen, not identified due to his age, faces several charges. They include weapons of mass destruction, criminal conspiracy, arson, and causing a catastrophe.

## RELATED ARTICLES
Euro 2016 terror fears: France on high alert

Police warn group of ISIS fighters en route to Europe

In February, a 15-year-old girl nearly killed an officer at Hanover train station by stabbing him in the neck with a kitchen knife. Afterward, security services called for a change in the law.

Police say they missed vital clues that the girl had turned to extremist Islam. These included a recent trip to Turkey, where she tried to cross into Syria to join Islamic State.

While there, prosecutors claim she met two ISIS recruiters who convinced her to carry out a "martyr operation" in Germany.

Included in the package of new security laws would be increased police powers to deploy undercover agents.

Buyers of pre-paid mobile phones, often used by terrorist gangs to evade surveillance, will have to provide ID and a home address.

Germany has been struck by a wave of terror attacks perpetrated by teenage fanatics

Germany has avoided a major attack by Islamist extremists. But, security services warn of ISIS-linked sleeper cells in the country.

It also served as a transit country for the militants who carried out the Paris and Brussels attacks.

Germany's Merkel says hopes Britain remains in EU

RELATED VIDEOS
Potential terrorist attack in Angel station?

Major terror alert in Brussels after suspect arrested near main...

French terrorist who killed police commander

Intelligence agencies say ISIS may have planted fighters among last year's migrants.

Marian Wendt, a member of Chancellor Merkel's conservatives, sits on the domestic affairs committee in the Bundestag. He told Reuters: "The heightened threat level has underscored the need to reduce hurdles for the German intelligence services, notably in the area of data retention where the law remains very restrictive compared to other European countries.""

RELATED ARTICLES
15-year-old boy arrested over terror fears

French police arrest suspect 'planning attacks on tourists'

JIHADIS IN UK: Shock as 400 trained ISIS fighters return from Syria

Part C

# Indonesian family that bombed churches well off, friendly

## By NINIEK KARMINI May 14, 2018 AP NEWS

A Muslim woman weeps at a wake for Sri Pudji Astutik, a victim of Sunday's church attacks. The wake was at a funeral home in Surabaya, East Java, Indonesia, on Monday, May 14, 2018. The bombings raised concerns about revived militant networks in Indonesia. They may have been reinvigorated by the return of some of the 1,100 Indonesians who fought with the Islamic State in Syria. Experts have warned for several years that when those fighters return, they could pose a significant threat. (AP Photo/Achmad Ibrahim)

SURABAYA, Indonesia (AP) — A Muslim family carried out suicide attacks on three churches in Indonesia's second-largest city, killing a dozen people and its two young daughters. They lived in an upper-middle-class suburb and were friendly with a Christian neighbor.

The coordinated bombings on Sunday, and a suicide attack on Monday by another family on police headquarters in Surabaya, have horrified Indonesians. They see their Muslim-majority country as diverse and tolerant.

Neighbors saw no signs the family planned the violence that President Joko "Jokowi" Widodo condemned as "barbaric" and "inhuman." They had lived in the leafy Wonorejo Asri community since 2010. Their neighbors said the father had a good business selling herbal medicines.

According to police, on Sunday morning the two sons, aged 16 and 18, rode a motorcycle into a church courtyard and detonated their explosives. Puji Kuswati, the mother, attacked worshippers at another church. Her 8 and 12-year-old daughters, all wearing suicide vests, did too, police said. The father, Dita Oepriarto, detonated a car bomb outside a third church. Police initially gave his name as Dita Futrianto but corrected that based on his national identity card. All six died.

Raith Yunanto, who lives two houses from the family, said they were always welcoming to her, a minority Christian. She said she went shopping with Kuswati at the local market and they often exchanged different types of food and fruit.

"There was nothing strange about the family, they were like other devout Muslim families," she said. "Their attitude and manner of dress were just like common Muslim people."

"It's difficult for us to accept how they can commit such a barbaric act against Christians," Yunanto said. "The couple visited me when I gave birth and when my children were sick."

She last saw the family on Saturday afternoon, before the bombings. The daughters were riding bicycles with other children in front of her house.

The eldest son, she said, was seen coming home from school activities. He wore a colourful batik shirt. It symbolizes Indonesia's diversity. The country has over 260 million people and many ethnic groups and languages.

Dendri Oemiarti, Oepriarto's younger sister, was grief-stricken. She spoke to The Associated Press on Monday. Her elderly parents were in shock.

"What he has done has hurt us so deeply," she said as tears flowed down her cheeks.

"What thoughts have influenced him? I do not understand. I do not know what changed my good brother to be so sadistic."

Oemiarti said she was very angry when she first heard about the church attacks and that children had been used to carry them out.

"I fainted when my sister, Dina, told me that the attack was done by our own brother," she said.

The last time she met her brother and his family was during Ramadan in 2017. She said their lives were busy and they only met about once a year and didn't talk about religion.

Police initially said the family went to Syria to join the Islamic State group but later retracted that statement.

Oepriarto, they said, was the leader of the Surabaya cell of Jemaah Anshorut Daulah, an Indonesian extremist group linked to IS.

Police say Oepriarto was friends with the family that bombed the police headquarters on Monday. He was also friends with a third family, three members of which died when homemade bombs exploded in their apartment on Sunday night.

The family's neighbor, Abi Akbar, said that Oepriarto and his sons, Yusuf and Firman, like most Muslim men in the neighborhood, usually attended dawn prayers at a local mosque. It was unremarkable.

But, Akbar, 23, heard older men in the community say that Oepriarto wasn't a mainstream Indonesian Muslim. They objected to secular rituals like raising the national flag and singing the national anthem.

In retrospect, Akbar said, one thing was different at dawn prayers on Sunday. Instead of customarily kissing their father's hand after prayers, the boys and father hugged for a long time.

"They hugged like they were going to be separated," Akbar said. "But at that time we were not suspicious of anything because they are a family that is well known and normal."

Just a few hours later Oepriarto and his family and 12 other people were dead. More than 40 were injured.

Kenzi Tapy Gani, a 21-year-old university student who lived near the family, described Oepriatro as a "friendly and nice guy." "We really didn't see it coming," he said. _

This story has been corrected to reflect new police information that youngest daughter's age was 8 not 9.

(The reality is throughout the world Terrorist are being supported by people who hide weapons in their homes or businesses. In Germany, there is a pattern of using homes near Mosques as safehouses. These same families will also faithfully indoctrinate their children as was demonstrated. The ones you never suspect are the most dangerous and unpredictable.

Glen R. Cook, 6)

# Muslim Children the World Over Indoctrinated in Hate

**by Raymond Ibrahim The Gatestone Institute April 6, 2021**

Originally published under the title "Indoctrinated in Hate: 'This Is the Start of the New Caliphate'."

Documentary filmmaker Alan Duncan recently visited the al-Hawl refugee camp in northeastern Syria, where children "are training ... for future jihad."

Boys throughout the Muslim world are increasingly indoctrinated into becoming super jihadis: ISIS 2.0. The news is coming in fast from a variety of sources.

A documentary filmmaker, Alan Duncan, made a short video of his visit to al-Hawl refugee camp in northeastern Syria. The camp is run by the Kurdish-led Syrian Democratic Forces. Although 80% of the camp consists of women and (27,000) children, many of whom had fled ISIS, the camp is known as the "Womb of ISIS."

In the video, highlighted in a February 2021 report, eight- to ten-year-old boys appear raising one finger — symbolic of jihad. When asked about the gesture, one boy responded: "This means the Islamic State remains." On being asked if they want to be doctors or teachers when they grow up, one boy says, "We don't want to be a doctor. We want to be a brother fighter. We want to fight the apostates." Then a woman, dressed in a black burka, declares that she wants the children to become "mujahidin who fight in the way Allah" — who "fight the infidels."

According to Duncan, the reason for all this indoctrination is that:

There are already training camps in there — they are training the ISIS ideologies to the kids. They are not teaching them A, B and C — they are teaching them to hate. To hate the West .... They are training them for future jihad.... The children are victims of ISIS and their parents. They are within an extremist Islamic-controlled camp. They are not being told how to become doctors and nurses — the little girls are there to serve and breed. The boys are there to be the future fighters and the future suicide bombers.... This is the start of the new caliphate. I am certain of it. You can sense the fear in there of the religious police. They are trying to keep the structure of caliphate in there — the laws, the punishment. It's like walking in the caliphate. It's like walking into another world.

A camp official agreed, adding:

The women and children are radicalized — the vehicles of the humanitarian workers are even attacked with stones. The guards do feel unsafe while patrolling the camp. However, they are armed and trained.

In Nigeria, Islamic terrorists released a 17-minute video. It showed children in "religious education and indoctrination sessions." A report on February 28, 2021, stated:

Boko Haram has released a video. It shows children as young as 10 being trained in combat. They called them the 'Next Generation Fighters.' In the alleged training video, the child soldiers are seen being trained with sophisticated weapons like AK-47 rifles and Zastava M21, a very powerful weapon... The images from the video show the relatively young children dressed in combat-style clothing and balaclava participating in martial arts training, weapon handling training and religious education class....

Hate-filled indoctrination takes place in schools all around the Muslim world.

Hate-filled indoctrination and training in violence is not limited to the "schools" of ISIS or Boko Haram. Public schools all around the Muslim world share elements of this indoctrination. A March 2021 study found that Turkey's school curriculum, once very secular, is now full of jihadi propaganda. Some of the report's "main findings" follow:

The Turkish curriculum has been significantly radicalized in recent years. Jihad war is introduced as a central value; martyrdom in battle is glorified. Islam is depicted as political, using science and technology to advance its goals. An ethno-nationalist religious vision combining neo-Ottomanism and pan-Turkism is taught. Concepts such as "Turkish World Domination" and Turkish or Ottoman "Ideal of the World Order" are emphasized. The curriculum is anti-American and sympathetic to ISIS and Al-Qaeda. There are anti-Armenian and pro-Azerbaijani stances. ... Subtle anti-democratic messaging is conveyed (e.g., Gezi Park protests). Christians and Jews are characterized as infidels instead of People of the Book.

The curriculum demonizes Zionism and verges on anti-Semitic.

Even in the West, online "virtually" during the pandemic, Muslim children are being indoctrinated. According to a March 4, 2021 report (updated March 10), "Children are being exposed to ISIS terrorism online during lockdown, raising fears of brainwashing, the British foreign secretary said." Dominic Raab told Parliament that "violent internet indoctrination" is rising at a "critical moment." Last year, terrorist propaganda increased by 7%. He added:

Terrorists can reach those most vulnerable to extremist ideas. And we can see a worrying rise in the proportion of children and teenagers that are now being arrested for terrorism offenses.

Raab called it a "perfect storm." It was a mix of "bored youths stuck indoors during lockdown," who are "subjected to extremist propaganda online."

There is another factor: an unprecedented radicalization of Muslim youth in jihadi hate and violence. It is occurring at a time when boys in the West are being indoctrinated to renounce masculinity and embrace effeminacy. In a few decades, what will happen when all these boys, raised on hate and violence and on total tolerance, become the world's decision-makers?

Raymond Ibrahim is the Judith Friedman Rosen Fellow at the Middle East Forum

+++++++++++++++++++++++++++++++++++++++++
++++++++++++++++++++++++++++++++++++

**Schools in Pakistan teach hatred against Hindus, Jews, Baloch activist told UN**

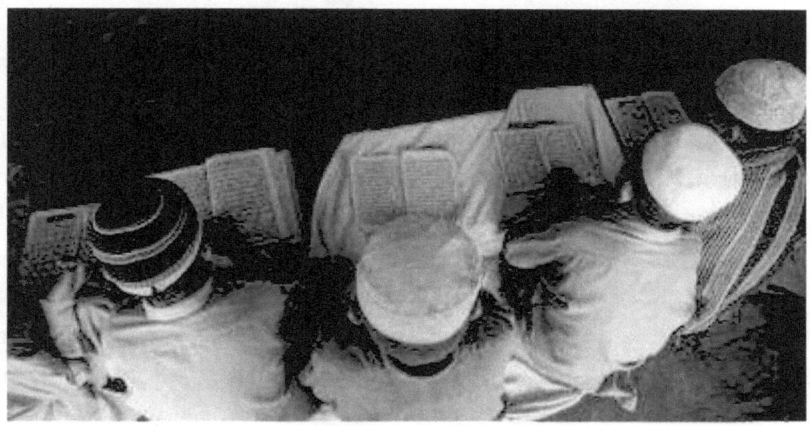

Munir Mengal, president of Baloch Voice Association

GENEVA: A Baloch activist told the UN that schools in Pakistan teach hatred of Hindus and Jews. While speaking at the UN in Geneva, Munir Mengal, president of the Baloch Voice Association, said, "I went to a very high-standard, state-run Army school called Cadet College." The first lesson was: Hindus are Kafirs, Jews are enemies of Islam. Both are liable to death for no other reason." He added, "Even today, the most important message from Army teachers is to respect guns and bombs. We must use them to kill Hindu mothers, or they will give birth to Hindu children." This sort of hatred is being taught in Pakistani schools, madrassas at every level even today. And is a basic part of the education syllabus. Munir told the UN Working Group that religious fanatics and terrorists are state strategic assets.

"Similarly, Blasphemy Law is being used to punish vulnerable religious minorities. It is a tool for discrimination." "In Pakistan, labeling someone a blasphemer is heroic. So is punishing the whole community and killing the accused," said the Baloch activist. "So is killing anyone who spoke against the misuse of the Blasphemy Law." He asks the UN to accept that neo-colonial states are suppressing humans. Without that, we can't create effective policies to protect against discrimination. Munir added, "Again I give the example of Balochistan, which was annexed by force against the will of people by the Islamic State of Pakistan. Now, under the "Mega Projects," "Economic Development Projects," and "port development projects," we have tactics to gain depth. They aim to expand and dominate. They are tools to eliminate and control people. These projects sound attractive, but they are not. A Baloch activist, a victim of Pakistan's brutal atrocities, told the UN, "In South Asia, everyone hears the ringing bells of CPEC, the China-Pakistan Economic Corridor, an economic development project." China also claimed that CPEC is the flagship project of her Belt and Road Initiative. But in reality, it is a high sign of neo colonisation, and expansionism. First, this all is being done without the consent of people. A large number of People were displaced forcibly. There are no jobs for local Baloch people. Even no drinking water for locals but you can see unimaginable facilities for Chinese people". He added, "Just imagine the current Population of Gawadar is 80,000 and Under CPEC there are plans to bring at least 500,000 Chinese people. This sort of altering demography means completely eliminating the Baloch race from that Area. Currently what tools the state has opted to achieve her objectives. Military operations, forced displacements, and barring media. Also, extrajudicial killings and forced disappearances. Speaking or writing against the state narrative is treachery. Hence Pakistan has profiled Baloch People as anti-development". Munir asked, "How will this group check states for discrimination? How to monitor neo-colonialism and state expansionism?"

**WATCHSchools in Pakistan teach hatred against Hindus and Jews: Baloch activist**

++++++++++++++++++++++++++++++++++++
+++++++++++++++++++++++++++

**Palestinians' Summer Camps To Kill Jews**

**by Bassam Tawil July 20, 2023 at 5:00 am**

For over a decade, the Iranian-backed groups Hamas and Islamic Jihad have run summer camps for thousands of schoolchildren in Gaza. These camps have spread an extreme ideology. It glorifies Jihad, terrorism, and armed struggle against Israel. The goal is to "liberate Palestine from the [Jordan] River to the [Mediterranean] Sea.""

The camps also provide military training. This includes knife and firearm practice, hand-to-hand combat, and marching drills. The children also stage plays and enact scenes of fighting and capturing Israeli soldiers or firing rockets at Israel.

On July 8, Hamas launched its summer camps for 2023, with the participation of more than 100,000 boys and girls.... The children are being trained to carry out terror attacks and serve as human shields in the Jihad against Israel.

In June 2022, Palestinian Authority Prime Minister Mohammad Shtayyeh denied any trace of Jewish history in Jerusalem...

When Hamas talks about "liberation," it is expressing its desire to eliminate Israel, as explicitly stated in the charter of the group:

"Article 11: The Islamic Resistance Movement holds that Palestine is an Islamic Waqf. It has been since ancient times and until the Day of Resurrection. No one can renounce or abandon any part of it.""

"Article 13: The Islamic Resistance Movement opposes peace initiatives, so-called peaceful solutions, and international conferences to resolve the Palestinian problem." For renouncing any part of Palestine means renouncing part of the religion...."

The summer camp director in Rafah, Muhammad Barhoum, said the camps are part of Hamas' focus on the younger generation. It is "the generation of liberation and victory."" — MEMRI, July 17, 2023

As in previous years, the summer camps focus on teaching the kids about various weapons. These include the AK-47, sniper rifles, RPGs, mortars, and machine guns. The campers practice assembling and disassembling the weapons, holding them and using them, and also train in urban warfare and tunnel warfare.... The camps present terrorists who killed Israelis as role models. Their portraits are in the camps and in camp activities. — MEMRI, July 17, 2023.

The spokesperson for the Hamas summer camps, Abu Bilal, said that... "the young people have [always] been the ones to carry out armed operations, and were the fuel of the intifadas and uprisings." — MEMRI, June 28, 2021.

This sweeping child abuse by Palestinians is ignored by the Western media, the United Nations and most politicians. Next time Palestinians complain about harm to minors in attacks on Israelis, remember the scenes of children in Gaza's summer camps. They are where the process to turn them into combatants begins.

The international community must hold Palestinian leaders accountable. Their training of children to be "martyrs" in a Jihad to kill Jews is child abuse. It also seeks to destroy the region's only democratic nation. Human rights organizations should lead this effort.

This summer, more than 100,000 Palestinian children in Gaza will attend summer camps run by Hamas and Islamic Jihad. The camps teach the children to fight Israel and Jews. They provide military training in knives, firearms, hand-to-hand combat, and marching drills. Pictured: Masked gunmen from Hamas' Izaddin al-Qassam Brigades register children for their summer camp, on June 14, 2021, in Gaza City. (Photo by Mahmud Hams/AFP via Getty Images)

While schoolchildren worldwide enjoy summer vacation, Palestinian kids are being taught to fight Israel and Jews.

The indoctrination and brainwashing of Palestinian children is not new. Palestinian leaders have been raising generation after generation on hatred for Israel and Jews. This incitement has gone on for decades in Palestinian kindergartens, schools, universities, mosques, the media, and even crossword puzzles. That is why, unsurprisingly, polls show many Palestinians support terrorism and radical views against Israel.

For over a decade, Hamas and Islamic Jihad, backed by Iran, have run summer camps for thousands of schoolchildren in Gaza. These camps aim to instill an extreme ideology. It glorifies Jihad (holy war), terrorism, and armed struggle against Israel. The goal is to "liberate Palestine from the [Jordan] River to the [Mediterranean] Sea.""

The camps also provide military training. This includes: knife and firearm practice, hand-to-hand combat, and marching and foot drills. The children also stage plays and enact scenes of fighting and capturing Israeli soldiers or firing rockets at Israel.

Hamas and Palestinian Islamic Jihad recruit for summer camps via their websites, social media, and booths in mosques and public places in Gaza. Their members staff the booths. Senior Hamas and Palestinian Islamic Jihad officials regularly attended the camps' opening and graduation ceremonies, where they gave speeches.

On July 8, Hamas <u>launched</u> its summer camps for 2023, with the participation of more than 100,000 boys and girls. This year›s summer camps are under the slogan Shield of Jerusalem. It implies that the terror group will use the children to fight Israel. The children are being trained to carry out <u>terror</u> attacks and serve as human shields in the Jihad against Israel. They are being taught that they are being recruited to take part in the battle to «<u>liberate</u>" Jerusalem. Needless to say, the Palestinians do not recognize Jews' rights and history in Jerusalem.

In June 2022, Palestinian Authority Prime Minister Mohammad Shtayyeh <u>denied</u> any trace of Jewish history in Jerusalem:

"We are on the outskirts of the eternal capital. It is the jewel in the crown, the point where heaven and earth meet, and the flower of all cities. It is the object of longing for both Muslims and Christians. They come to pray in the Al-Aqsa Mosque and walk the Via Dolorosa to the Church of the Holy Sepulchre. This church witnessed the signing of the Pact of Umar. In it, the Caliph Umar promised the people of Iliya [Arabic for Aelia Capitolina/Jerusalem] that no Muslim would pray in their church." [Jerusalem] has Canaanite, Roman, Islamic, and Christian antiquities and is theirs alone, and no one else has any traces in it."

Khaled Abu Askar, head of Hamas's Summer Camps Committee, said at a Gaza press conference in Asdaa Entertainment City, near Khan Yunis:

"We meet today in Asdaa City. It has simulations of some Jerusalem landmarks. We announce the launch of our summer camps, the Quds [Jerusalem] Shield camps." Let us assure the world that the city of Jerusalem, with its sanctities, is the compass of every free and honorable Palestinian."

Abu Askar claimed that Hamas cares about the young generation and is keen to invest in them. He also claimed that young Palestinians are being targeted. This is to undermine their beliefs, behavior, morals, and patriotism. Whom does he blame? Israel, of course.

"They are spending a lot to divert the youth from their religion and homeland," he said. A Hamas official said his group named its camps "Jerusalem Shield" to instill the value of Jerusalem in young people. It aims to promote their right to the Holy City and the liberation generation's national role, and to raise their resolve."

When Hamas talks about "liberation," it is expressing its desire to eliminate Israel, as explicitly stated in the charter of the group:

"Article 11: The Islamic Resistance Movement holds that Palestine is an Islamic Waqf. It has been since ancient times, and until the Day of Resurrection. No one can renounce, part with, or abandon any of it." No Arab country, nor all of them together, has that right. Neither do any Arab kings or presidents, nor all of them together. Nor does any organization, or all of them together, be they Palestinian or Arab.

Palestine is an Islamic Waqf through all generations, to the Day of Resurrection.

"Article 13: The Islamic Resistance Movement rejects peace initiatives. They oppose so-called peaceful solutions and international conferences to resolve the Palestinian problem." To renounce any part of Palestine is to renounce part of the religion. The Islamic Resistance Movement's nationalism is part of its faith. The movement teaches its members to fight their Jihad and raise Allah's banner over their homeland. "Allah is all-powerful, but most people are unaware."

At another ceremony in the Gaza Strip, Jum'a Hassanein, chairman of the Rafah Administrative Committee, said, "These youth camps aim to train a generation of liberation and victory."

The summer camp director in Rafah, Muhammad Barhoum, said the camps are part of Hamas' efforts on the younger generation. They are "the generation of liberation and victory.""

The summer camps, like in previous years, will teach the kids to use various weapons. These include the AK-47, sniper guns, RPG launchers, mortars, and machine guns. The campers practice assembling and disassembling the weapons. They also train in urban and tunnel warfare. Some of the lessons are taught by masked members of Hamas' armed wing, the 'Izz Al-Din Al-Qassam Brigades, and some are even held in Hamas military bases. A boy at one of the camps demonstrated tunnel warfare for Younis Al-Astal, a Hamas member of the Palestinian Legislative Council. He was touring the camps with other Hamas officials. At some of the camps, Israeli flags were spread on the ground so that the campers would step on them. The camps present terrorists who attacked Israelis as role models. Their portraits are in the camps and in camp activities."

Hamas spokesperson Abdel Latin Qanou said that the group's summer camps in Gaza are an important step. They aim to build this generation and instill in them a love for Jerusalem and the Al-Aqsa Mosque. The camps link them to their "legitimate right to return [to

Israel] and liberation." Qanou stated that the slogan "Shield of Jerusalem" aims to prepare the children for "liberating Jerusalem.""

In the past, Palestinian Islamic Jihad held summer camps. They were called Revenge of the Free. Hundreds of boys under 17 participated.

Darwish al-Gharabli, a leader of Palestinian Islamic Jihad, said during a graduation ceremony:

"These camps create a generation that supports Jihad and resistance. They believe in fighting for Palestine and see it as a holy duty to fight the Jews." Our jihad against this continues in all arenas. We assure our enemy that this generation will carry the banner and resist with all strength."

In 2021, Hamas's armed wing, Izz al-din al-Qassam Brigades, held summer camps under the slogan Sword of Jerusalem.

The Izz al-Din al-Qassam Brigades' website says, "The camps aim to spark jihad in the youth, instill Islamic values, and prepare an army to liberate Palestine."

Hamas summer camps' spokesperson, Abu Bilal, said they are held "out of belief in the role of the young people and a sense of responsibility for the [younger] generation." He added that "the young people have [always] been the ones to carry out armed operations, and were the fuel of the intifadas and uprisings.""

This sweeping child abuse by Palestinians is ignored by the Western media, the United Nations and most politicians. Next time Palestinians complain about minors being killed in attacks on Israelis, recall the scenes from the Gaza Strip's summer camps. They are where children are transformed into combatants.

The international community, especially human rights groups, must hold Palestinian leaders accountable for child abuse. They train children to be "martyrs" in a Jihad to kill Jews and destroy the region's only democracy.

*Bassam Tawil is a Muslim Arab based in the Middle East.*

Author's Note: "Do not think Christians will be left out because Jesus Christ was a Jew" to quote a Moslem Shop Owner in Cairo..

# Taliban reverses decision, barring Afghan girls from attending school beyond 6th grade

**Updated March 23, 20222:27 PM ET  Heard on** <u>All Things Considered</u>
**By  Fazelminallah Qazizai**

*Girls enter a school before class in Kabul on Sept. 12, 2021. In a surprise decision, Afghanistan's new hardline rulers will not allow girls to attend school beyond sixth grade.*
*Felipe Dana/AP*

KABUL, Afghanistan — In a morning of tears and anger, the Taliban broke their promise to allow Afghan girls to attend secondary school. Thousands of girls, in their uniforms and carrying school bags, turned up at their old school gates.

## WORLD
### As school resumes in Afghanistan, will all girls be allowed to go?

The sudden change raised fears the Taliban would deny girls an education. When the militant religious movement first ruled Afghanistan from 1996 to 2001, girls were not allowed to study.

"Some of my classmates began weeping," said Sakina Jafari, an 18-year-old who hoped to resume her year 11 classes. "We were so excited to return. And now we don't know what will happen to us."

Another young woman who spoke to Afghan news outlet TOLO burst into tears. She had waited 186 days, and had counted, for school to resume. They had turned her away. "What is our crime? That we are girls?" she raged.

The Taliban faced widespread condemnation. They did not say when to expect the classrooms to reopen. Most girls and young women have been prevented from attending secondary school since the Taliban swept to power in August.

Afghanistan's new rulers reopened schools for boys, and for girls up to the 6th grade. **They then allowed women to attend college. But, it was under strict segregation from male students and a rigidly-enforced dress code.** But secondary school remained off limits.

However, Taliban officials said Monday they would allow all students, including secondary girls, to attend classes starting Wednesday, the Afghan new year. But just as the girls turned up to their school gates, they were sent home by Taliban officials who told them to wait for an official announcement.

One senior official insisted the Taliban had not reneged but needed more time to decide on a school uniform for teenage girls.

"There's no issue with banning girls from schools," said Suhail Shaheen, the Taliban's UN ambassador-designate, in response to NPR. "It is only a technical issue of deciding on form of school uniform for girls. We hope the uniform issue is resolved and finalized as soon as possible."

That was echoed by one Kabul school teacher, who requested anonymity because she didn't want to anger Taliban officials. She said that, as girls entered her classroom, the principal stopped them. She said, "'Don't come in here until we've got official permission." And when you come back, you have to wear a black face veil, a black chador and a black scarf.'"

The teacher says her students were distressed. They argued that they were wearing modest clothes already – loose shirts and pants and headscarves. "One of them said, 'we are ready to wear burkas but please let us stay,'" she recalled one young woman pleading. "But we told them they had to leave."

An article on the pro-Taliban Bakhtar News Agency, which celebrated the return of students to school, reported that the Education Ministry's spokesman, Mawlawi Aziz Ahmad Ryan, said, "schools for women from the sixth grade above are closed until further notice.'"

Ryan said a plan would be formulated "in accordance with Islamic law and Afghan culture and traditions, as well as the ruling of the Islamic Emirate."

*Afghan students leave classes in a primary school in Kabul, on March 27, 2021.*
*Rahmat Gul/AP*

In the Muslim world, "culture and traditions" often means imposing rules. These rules deny women their Islamic rights, as local culture does not permit it. Islamic teaching and practice encourages men and women to study and learn.

Western countries want girls to return to school. It's a key condition for restarting aid to Afghanistan. These donors largely cut off aid after the U.S. withdrew from Afghanistan and the Taliban seized power. For others, allowing Afghan girls to receive an education is a prerequisite for recognizing the Taliban's rule.

"I deeply regret today's announcement by Taliban authorities in Afghanistan. "They have suspended girls' education from the sixth grade until further notice," said U.N. Secretary-General António Guterres. "I urge the Taliban de facto authorities to open schools for all students without any further delay."

## CONSIDER THIS FROM NPR
### In A New Afghanistan, Some Women Fear For
### Their Rights — But Others Are Hopeful

The U.S. Chargé d'Affaires Ian McCary tweeted that he was "deeply troubled" by the policy reversal.

Nobel Peace Prize laureate Malala Yousafzai was shot in the face by a Taliban fighter in Pakistan for advocating for girls' education. She said she was disappointed. "I had one hope for today: that Afghan girls walking to school would not be sent back home. But the Taliban did not keep their promise. "They will find excuses to stop girls from learning. They are afraid of educated girls and empowered women," she said.

**The decision reflects reported splits in the Taliban's leadership**

The Taliban's sudden change shows an internal debate. Analysts say it is over whether girls should attend high school at all.

Those divisions are exemplified by a tweet from Ahmad Yasir, the deputy head from the office of the first deputy prime minister. He wrote that he saw no religious justification for girls not to attend school, but subsequently deleted the tweet.

Heather Barr of Human Rights Watch studies women's rights in Afghanistan. She says the latest news "is absolutely devastating."

She said she feared it may signal a repeat of when the Taliban did not allow girls to attend school when they ruled Afghanistan from 1996 to 2001.

It was then that the Taliban said closing schools for girls was "a temporary situation," Barr said.

"And they would allow girls to study ... once conditions were right," she said.

But that moment never arrived," Barr said. "And today it feels like it will never arrive this time either."

Hadid reported from Islamabad; Qazizai reported from Kabul.

**Afghan Girls National Soccer Team—Banned Under The Taliban—Granted Asylum With Their Families By Portugal**

Téa Kvetenadze Forbes Staff Sep 21, 2021,05:02pm EDT Updated Sep 22, 2021, 10:45am EDT

Portugal granted asylum to the Afghan girls national soccer team and their families. They arrived in Lisbon on Sunday after weeks on the run from the Taliban, which has banned women from playing sports. The Associated Press first reported this on Tuesday.

Farkhunda Muhtaj, the captain of the Afghanistan women's national soccer team, top center, is seen ... [+] ASSOCIATED PRESS

KEY FACTS

The group of 80 included the 26 players, aged between 14 and 16, and their family members.

They had been trying to leave Afghanistan for weeks after the U.S. withdrawal and the Taliban's takeover in August. But, they had no success.

The team found out they were leaving early Sunday and were evacuated via chartered plane within hours.

"Operation Soccer Balls" was a collaboration of several groups. It included U.S. allies, humanitarian networks, and even the Taliban.

Most of the national women's team players were evacuated to Australia in August.

## CRUCIAL QUOTE

"They left their homes and left everything behind," Farkhunda Muhtaj told the AP. Muhtaj is the Canadian-based captain of the Afghan women's team, and helped coordinate the rescue. "They can't fathom that they're out of Afghanistan."

## KEY BACKGROUND

The team had been moving between safehouses ever since the Taliban took control of Afghanistan last month. Despite vague Taliban promises to preserve women's rights, they've banned girls from playing sports. They've also replaced the Women's Affairs Ministry with the "Ministry for Promotion of Virtue and Prevention of Vice." These are among other concerning developments.

## FURTHER READING

"Afghanistan girls soccer team given asylum in Portugal" (The Associated Press)

"Effort underway to rescue girls soccer team from Afghanistan" (The Associated Press)

"Taliban Use Tear Gas, Fire Into Air To Break Up Women's March" (Forbes)

**Téa Kvetenadze**

# The 'Right' to Rape and Enslave Non-Muslim Women

## by <u>Raymond Ibrahim</u> June 14, 2023 at 5:00 am

*Last month, in Fra*nce, a Muslim man told an underage girl with whom he had been chatting on Facebook, "I will burn you all. I will cut your throats. I will rape you and your mother because I have the right to do so."

The girl's father, described as "devastated and angry," responded to the terror threats with which his family and he had been living, saying, "Islam is not what I have been hearing [it is]... Religion is peace, tolerance, respect... We have been living in fear for a year!"

The ongoing narrative is that Islam means peace; what is not said is that this peace comes only *after* everyone enjoys the «peace» of being Muslim. Until then, what is often presented to hasten this result is the exact opposite: jihad, or violence in the service of Islam. Many Muslims, just want, of course, to live in quiet lives, have good jobs and enjoy the blessings of this life. Some, like Western converts to the «religion of peace,» become terrorists. This is sudden and inexplicable.

Such men routinely cite the same *hadiths* and verses from the Koran. Verses 4:3 and 4:24 permit Muslim men to have sex with as many women as «their right hand possesses.» This means, of course, all non-Muslim women they can capture in a jihad.

"In the moments before he raped the 12-year-old girl, the Islamic State fighter took the time to explain that what he was about to do was not a sin. "The Quran gave him the right to rape her, he insisted. It not only allowed it, but also encouraged it, because she practiced a religion other than Islam."" [Emphasis added] —*New York Times* report.

In Germany, some Muslim migrants act out their conviction that all "German women are there for sex." In the 2016 New Year's celebrations in Cologne, migrants ended up molesting a thousand women.

In Britain, a large Muslim minority has long existed. In various regions, thousands of British girls have been abused and gang-raped by "grooming gangs." These gangs, largely made up of Muslims, apparently deemed it their Islamic right. One rape victim said, "The men who did this to me have no remorse. They would tell me that what they were doing was OK in their culture."

In a separate case, a convicted Muslim rapist told a British court that sharing non-Muslim girls for sex "was part of Somali culture" and "a religious requirement."

The West will see, as "exotic," the subhuman treatment and sexual degradation of non-Muslim women and children by Muslim men who deem it their "right.""

In Britain, a large Muslim minority has long existed. In various regions, thousands of British girls have been abused and gang-raped by "grooming gangs." These gangs, mostly made up of Muslims, apparently deemed it their Islamic right. Pictured: The English town of Rotherham (population ca. 265,000), where at least 1,400 children were sexually abused by a gang of Muslim men of Pakistani descent. (Image source: Wikimedia Commons)

Last month, in France, a Muslim man told an underage girl with whom he had been chatting on Facebook, «I will burn you all. I will cut your throats. I will rape you and your mother because I have the right to do so.»

When she refused to marry him, he made even more severe threats. At one point, he texted, "Soon we will cut your throats and play football with your heads." It included a video of a beheading.

Based on the name given in the French report, Fabio Califano, who was subsequently arrested, appears to have been a convert to Islam.

The girl's father, described as "devastated and angry," responded to the terror threats with which his family and he had been living, saying, "Islam is not what I have been hearing [it is]... Religion is peace, tolerance, respect... We have been living in fear for a year!"

The ongoing narrative is that Islam means peace; what is not said is that this peace comes only *after* everyone enjoys the "peace" of being Muslim. Until then, what is often presented to hasten this result is the exact opposite: jihad, or violence in the service of Islam. Many Muslims, just want, of course, to live in quiet lives, have good jobs and enjoy the blessings of this life. Others however, such as Western converts to the «religion of peace» suddenly and inexplicably become terrorists.

Unfortunately, assertions such as "we will cut your throats and play football with your heads" echo through the ages. Mu'izzi, an eleventh century Persian poet for instance, tried to incite an emir to butcher all Christians in the Middle East:

"For the Arab religion, it is a duty, O ghazi king, to clear Syria of patriarchs and bishops, and Rum [Anatolia] of priests and monks." You should kill those accursed dogs and wretched creatures... You should... cut their throats... You should make polo-balls of the Franks' heads in the desert, and polo sticks from their hands and feet."

[Hillenbrand, Carole, Turkish Myth and Muslim Symbol: The Battle of Manzikert, Edinburgh: Edinburgh University Press, 2007, 151–152.]

The line, however, that jumps out in the quote from Califano is: "I will rape you and your mother *because I have the right to do so*."

Importantly, it is not the first time that a Muslim man insists that he has the "right" — given by Islam — to enslave and rape non-Muslim women.

Such men routinely cite the same *hadiths* and verses from the Koran. Verses 4:3 and 4:24, for instance, permit Muslim men to have sex with as many women as «their right hand possesses.» This means, of course, as many non-Muslim women as they can capture during a jihad.

Koran 4:3: "If you fear you cannot be fair to orphans, then marry women you like, two, three, or four. If you fear you cannot be just between them, then marry only one or what your right hands possess. This is better, so you do not stray from the right path."" [Shakir translation]

Koran 4:24: "And all married women, except those whom your right hands possess. This is Allah's ordinance to you. All other women are lawful for you, provided you seek them with your property, taking them in marriage, not committing fornication." "Then, for those you profit by, give them their due dowries. There is no blame for what you mutually agree after that. Surely, Allah is Knowing, Wise."" [Shakir translation]

The Koran uses language, discussed here, that presents such women as *things*, not persons. Koran 4:3, translated literally, permits Muslims to copulate with "what"—not "who"—"your right hands possess." This is in Shakir's translation.

"...but if you fear that you will not do justice (between them), then (marry) only one or *what* your right hands possess (Koran 4:3).

(Click here and here for more Muslim scriptures that advocate sex-slavery.)

To see how these scriptures and terms shape the jihadist mind, consider excerpts from a New York Times report, "ISIS Enshrines a Theology of Rape.""

In the moments before he raped the 12-year-old girl, the Islamic State fighter took the time to explain that what he was about to do was not a sin. The Quran, he insisted, gave him the right to rape her. It condoned and encouraged it, since she practiced a religion other than Islam.

He bound her hands and gagged her. Then he knelt beside the bed and prostrated himself in prayer before getting on top of her.

When it was over, he knelt to pray again, bookending the rape with acts of religious devotion.

"I kept telling him it hurts — please stop," said the girl, whose body is so small an adult could circle her waist with two hands. "*He told me that according to Islam he is allowed to rape an unbeliever.* "*He said that by raping me, he is drawing closer to God," she said in a refugee camp here. She escaped there after 11 months of captivity.* [Emphases added.]

The report continues:

A 34-year-old Yazidi woman was bought and repeatedly raped by a Saudi fighter in the Syrian city of Shadadi. She fared better than the second slave, a 12-year-old girl, who was raped for days despite heavy bleeding.

"He destroyed her body. She was badly infected. The fighter kept coming and asking me, 'Why does she smell so bad?' And I said, she has an infection on the inside, you need to take care of her," the woman said.

Unmoved, he ignored the girl's agony, *continuing the ritual of praying before and after raping the child.*

"I said to him, 'She's just a little girl,' " the older woman recalled. "And he answered: 'No. She's not a little girl. She's a slave. And she knows exactly how to have sex.' "

*"And having sex with her pleases God," he said.*

The mainstream media and pundits say these beliefs have "nothing to do with Islam." But, they permeate Muslim society. Some may assume such beliefs are limited to ISIS and fanatical jihadists. But, evidence suggests otherwise.

In Pakistan, for example, three Christian girls were walking home after work. They were accosted by four "rich and drunk" Muslims in a car. They were hardly candidates for ISIS. They "misbehaved," yelled "suggestive and lewd comments," and harassed the girls to get in their car for "a ride and some fun." The girls declined the "invitation." They said they were "devout Christians and did not practice sex outside of marriage." The men became enraged and chased them. "How dare you run away from us," the men yelled. "Christian girls are only meant for one thing: the pleasure of Muslim men." The men then drove their car into the three girls, killing one and severely injuring the other two.

In a separate incident, a human rights activist spoke about a Muslim man's rape of a 9-year-old Christian girl. He revealed that

"Such incidents occur frequently. Christian girls are considered *goods to be damaged at leisure. Abusing them is a right.* According to the community's mentality it is not even a crime. Muslims regard them as *spoils of war.*" [Emphasis added.]

Most recently, a June 3, 2023 report detailed the suffering many Hindus experience as «infidels» in Pakistan, and quotes some who fled:

"In Pakistan, there is no difference between meat and women.... Had we stayed back, our women would have been torn to shreds."

Once limited to third world countries like Pakistan and ISIS areas, the abuse of "infidel" women is now common in the West.

In Germany, some Muslim migrants act out their conviction that all "German women are there for sex." In the 2016 New Year's celebrations in Cologne, migrants ended up molesting a thousand women.

In Britain, a large Muslim minority has long existed. Thousands of British girls have been abused and gang-raped by "grooming gangs" made up largely of Muslims. The gangs apparently deemed it their Islamic right. One rape victim said:

"The men who did this to me have no remorse. They would tell me that what they were doing was OK in their culture."

A Muslim imam in Britain confessed that Muslim men are taught that women are "second-class citizens, little more than chattels." They have "absolute authority" over them. The imams preach a doctrine that "denigrates all women" and holds whites, or non-Muslims, in "particular contempt.""

In a separate case, a convicted Muslim rapist told a British court that sharing non-Muslim girls for sex "was part of Somali culture" and "a religious requirement.""

Some "pious" Muslims see it as a "religious requirement." An ISIS rapist cited this to his 12-year-old victim. Others see it as part of the Islamic cultures of Pakistan, Somalia, and French converts. It is a brutal, "exotic" practice. The West is expected to embrace it for the sake of multiculturalism.

Raymond Ibrahim, author of Defenders of the West and Sword and Scimitar, is a fellow at two institutes. He is the Distinguished Senior Shillman Fellow at the Gatestone Institute. He is also the Judith Rosen Friedman Fellow at the Middle East Forum.

# Polygamy and the Results

Polygamy has a number of issues that drive the societal acceptance of the institution. By the same token, Polygamy has an equal number of drawbacks depending on a variety of factors.

The factors vary from the birth ratio to societal consequences of war to political power to polyandry to name a few. Some are easy to explain, such as polyandry in Nepal. Women have multiple husbands because land ownership is through the wife. This keeps farms sizeable and prosperous.)

Let's tackle the birth ratio first. One hundred six to one hundred three males to one hundred females. In China, in one community, it was one hundred seventy-five males to one hundred women. Two parts of this was the one child rule and secondly, abortion was and is a war on women and female babies. If you want a good understanding of what is happening to our population, look up Universe-25 by Dr. John Calhoun.

Next consider the decimation of war as applied to sex. War traditionally decimates the male population. To restore it, you must force multiple partners. If women were larger share of the casualties, there would be no restoring the population. This is also why verses 4.3 and 4.24 are important-right hand possess. Add to that the catastrophic damage a woman receives from the Haafud. The Moslem male looks for a partner who can respond, in other words one who is NOT a recipient of the Haafud. Since polygamy cuts the pool of women, the Moslem male must look outside of Islam. Political or Social prestige also play their part. One final point. With four wives for every man, 75% of males will be single. That excess testosterone will cause strife, terrorism, and pedophilia.

One other factor is the time factor in breeding. The male role is three minutes, and he is done. The woman's role only starts at three minutes or an hour or so. Then we add nine months of pregnancy. Then, we raise the baby for sixteen to eighteen years. The goal is to make them a capable adult in the adult world. This time factor again interferes with the ratio between the sexes. Also, is the Father even present or around? Remember, both the women and the children are property of the Father, or Grandfather.

Finally, in the animal kingdom, in many large mammal species, the males compete to have the largest selection of females. This is true in Seals, Wildebeests, Walruses among others as the Author understands it. A large number of males cannot breed, like in the Islamic World. So, they must fight anyone, including other Islamic sects, for breeding females.

Now couple that with religious upbringing. What can you tell me about the madrassa curriculum at the Dar Es Salaam school? Or any other? For example, are you okay with your ignorance, especially if you are a woman? Ask the Yazidi and Christians from Syria about it:

**Palestine, United States | Special Dispatch No. 10613**

**Introduction**

On May 6, 2023, the Leaders Academy in Philadelphia posted a video to its YouTube channel. It showed a performance by students of Palestinian heritage at the academy's "One Ummah Day" event. In the video, schoolgirls are seen singing and acting out a song praising "brave" Palestinian girls who are the sisters and daughters of "real men." In one part, the song describes a grandmother who arms her granddaughters with a stone and sells her jewelry in order to purchase firearms. Another part of the song describes a girl sending her brother off to battle. She tells him, "I will saddle your horse and tie a dagger to your belt – enhance your resolve." The Alhidaya Islamic Center in Philadelphia posted the video to its Facebook page. It is affiliated with Leaders Academy.

In 2019, a Philadelphia Islamic school posted clips of children singing about chopping heads. After MEMRI exposed this, the school removed the clip, claiming it hadn't been vetted. In 2017, the school posted a similar song.

The Philadelphia chapter of the Muslim American Society (MAS) posted on Facebook videos of young students singing "Chop off their heads!"" at the Leaders Academy's "One Ummah Day" events in 2017 and 2019." and expressed their willingness to become martyrs for the sake of Palestine and the Al-Aqsa Mosque.

On May 3, 2019, MEMRI released a clip from a video of an April 22, 2019, "Ummah Day" celebration at the Muslim American Society Islamic Center in Philadelphia (MAS Philly). The video was posted on the MAS Philly Facebook page. (See MEMRI TV clip no. 7194). The clip received over two million views on social media, and was denounced by Members of Congress. Following the release of the MEMRI clip, MAS Philly removed the video from its Facebook page.

*Screenshot from the 2019 video posted by the Muslim American Society Islamic Center in Philadelphia (MAS Philly).*

After MEMRI exposed these videos, Facebook suspended MAS Philadelphia's page. The MAS website no longer lists the Philadelphia chapter. See MEMRI Special Dispatch No. 8054 for more information about the public response to these clips. On May 15, 2019, MAS Philadelphia and Leaders Academy issued a statement. It said a «process» is in place to prevent an «unintended mistake.» A May 28, 2017, video on MAS Philly›s Facebook page showed children singing about their willingness to be martyred on Palestinian soil. (See MEMRI TV clip no. 7201).

*Screenshot from the 2017 video posted by the Muslim American Society Islamic Center in Philadelphia (MAS Philly).*

## In May 2023 Video, Children Sing About Girls, Women Arming 'Brave' Palestinian Fighters

Below is the transcript of a video on the Leaders Academy's YouTube channel. It shows students performing at the academy's 2023 "One Ummah Day" event. The Alhidaya Islamic Center in Philadelphia posted the video to its Facebook page. Leaders Academy is affiliated with the center.

***To view the clip, click <u>here</u> or below:***

**Girls:** "By Allah, I am a brave Palestinian, the sister and daughter of real men. I am Palestinian. My grandmother is a beautiful old woman, she armed us with a stone. She sold her Jewelry and bracelets and bought guns from the money.

"By Allah, I am a brave Palestinian, the sister and daughter of real men. I am Palestinian. [...]

"My brother, I will saddle up your horse, and I will tie a dagger to your belt. I am the star that lights up your night, enhance your resolve, and gird your loins.

"By Allah, I am a brave Palestinian, the sister and daughter of real men. I am Palestinian.

"My veil is the most beautiful *kaffiyeh*. I am brave, I am the sister and daughter of real men. There are glances of victory in my eyes. I am Palestinian."

### LATEST REPORTS
July 17, 2023

Hamas summer camps for children and teens in Gaza train them to use weapons. The goal is to raise a generation to liberate Palestine.

Who thinks the shooting at Marjorie Stoneman Douglas High School by Nicolas Cruz was not a bad idea? When I asked this question of the Broward County school board, only one person responded. Try this for a timeline: When is Ramadan? March to April. Followed with Jewish American Heritage month and Moslem Pride month, May. Let's stoke the fires. In June we have the Pride ( five gallons of kerosene) Month. Understand what I mean by stoke the fires. Have you even see the curriculum of the Madrassas or the Moslem calendar? What are the kids learning in summer camp? What do you American Islamic schools are like the sample that I showed you? By the way, Moslems like to return the scenes of past triumphs in hopes of repeating the success. Is Broward ready for a second MSD shootout under the current school board leadership of Lori Alhadeff? While it was not a Moslem shooter, it was a strike against the Islamic enemy? A 14-year-old, wannabe martyr in Germany was caught. His parents checked his email and notified the police. He had converted online. And this was before women had even entered the equation. These are the end results!

# Islam Quiz

Define Taqiya.

What is the difference between a Mufti, a Sheik and an Imam?

What is meant by the phrase "that which my right hand possesses?

What is meant by Tawriya?

Who are the children of the book?

Why do people who support Islam endorse pedophilia?

Why do people who endorse Islam support slavery?

How many people have been killed by Muslim expansionism?
2 million b. 20 million c. 200 million d. more than 200 million

What was the predominate culture in North Africa in 800 AD?

What is the Jadziya?

What is the genetic time bomb, caused by Islam? It is behind over 90% of genetic issues found almost exclusively in the Mideast. It is now spreading.

# Islam Quiz Answers

Define Taqiya. What ever benefits me benefits Islam if I am a believer and so is alright.

What is the difference between a Mufti and a Sheik and an Imam? Think Post Doctorate, Doctorate, Masters on a grand scale, and BA on a local scale in Islam.

What is meant by the phrase "that which my right hand possesses? Slaves

What is meant by Tawriya? Creative Lying

Who are the children of the book? Christians

Why do people who support Islam endorse pedophilia? Because the "prophet" had a six year old wife

Why do people who endorse Islam support slavery? Islam means Submit.

How many people have been killed by Muslim expansionism? D. more than 200 million

What was the predominate culture in North Africa in 800 AD? Berber Christian

What is the Jadziya? The tax on anyone who is not Muslim and is another faith and can be levied by any Muslim on a non-muslim.

What is the genetic time bomb, caused by Islam, that is spreading? It is responsible for over 90% of genetic problems found almost exclusively in the Mideast. Marriage of first cousins

# The Holy Books

Mein Kampf, Quran, Bible, Torah, Bhagavad Gita, and the Tipitaka
The Buddhist holy book is called the **Tipitaka,** which means "three baskets". It is a collection of the works of Buddha's teachings, preserved in an ancient Indian language called Pali. The Tipitaka is extremely large and consists of three main sections: the Vinaya Pitaka, the Sutta Pitaka, and the Abhidhamma Pitaka . The English translation of the entire Tipitaka fills up about forty volumes.

A look at the Holy Books of various religions and the texts of political groups reveals some key elements.

First, all the major Religion's Holy Books are written by more than one man. This is especially true in the Judeo-Christian World (Torah, Bible, Book of Mormon), the Buddhist "Tipitaka," and Hindu texts (Bhagavad Gita, Holy Book of Hindus, Tibetan Book of the Dead).

Political volumes are the work of one man's point of view that may be elaborated on like Karl Marx, Lennin, Muhammad, Mao, and Hitler. Hitler's "Mein Kampf" gave us Nazi philosophy. Muhammad's "Quran" gave us Islam and endless suffering for Infidels. Marx's "Das Kapital," Lenin's "What Is to Be Done?", and Mao's "Little Red Book" all gave us communism.

Further, if one compares Muhammad to Hitler, they both share certain similar viewpoints. Among the points that stand out are a barbaric legal code, a hatred of both Jewish and Christian beliefs, and a tyrannical, deceptive use of power. Their followers revere both religions' founders as prophets.

One thing that is almost impossible for most followers to do is to remove the blinders that the Religion installs like blinders on a horse. The thing to remember is a Religion is a free choice while political organizations are not as a general rule. You leave or join a religion as to what your heart's desire is. A political organization always has its hands on the levers of power through the use of laws. A political organization can and will use its power against anyone who does not support leadership goals. For an example, you have only to look at the Biden Presidency.

A political organization does not tolerate free thought as opposed to forced choice. An example is prayer five times a day for brainwashing or the new reading requirement in North Korea. Most tyrannical political groups see women as baby factories. They view political opponents as potential slaves.

Remember the choice is yours, chose wisely.

# The Defense: Islam vs. the Constitution

The issue is: **Islam's belief in Sharia vs. The Christian Belief of the Constitution.**

**The problem is the OATH of Office.**

**OATH REFERENCES:**

**PRESIDENT All oaths of public office begin: "I do solemnly swear (or affirm) that I will faithfully execute the Office of President of the United States, and will to the best of my ability, preserve, protect and defend the Constitution of the United States.""**

**MILITARY ENLISTED: "I, _____, do solemnly swear (or affirm) that I will support and defend the Constitution of the United States against all enemies, foreign and domestic; that I will bear true faith and allegiance to the same; and that I will obey the orders of the President of the United States and the orders of the officers appointed over me, according to regulations and the Uniform Code of Military Justice. So, help me God."**

**MILITARY OFFICER: "I, _____ (SSAN), having been appointed an officer in the _____ (Military Branch) of the United States, as indicated above in the grade of _____ do solemnly swear (or affirm) that I will support and defend the Constitution of the United States against all enemies, foreign or domestic, that I will bear true faith and allegiance to the same; that I take this obligation freely, without any mental reservation or purpose of evasion; and that I will well and faithfully discharge the duties of the office upon which I am about to enter; So help me God."**

**JUDGE "I, ___ ___, do solemnly swear (or affirm) that I will administer justice without respect to persons, and do equal right to the poor and to the rich, and that I will faithfully and impartially discharge and perform all the duties incumbent upon me as ___ under the Constitution and laws of the United States. So, help me God." Or Congress, CONGESS - SENATE AND HOUSE OF REPRESENTATIVES**

**"I do solemnly swear (or affirm) that I will support and defend the Constitution of the United States against all enemies, foreign and domestic; that I will bear true faith and allegiance to the same;** that I take this obligation freely, without any mental reservation or purpose of evasion; and that I will well and faithfully discharge the duties of the office on which I am about to enter: So help me God."

Do we detect a common theme of defending or a vested interest in the Constitution? The question then becomes what is the threat to the Constitution? That is what this trial must be about. That question has to be preceded by a question of what does the bedrock of the Constitution depend on? That answer is the Constitution revolves around the ninth Commandment. You shall not bear false witness **Bible reference - Exodus 20:15:** *"You shall not bear false witness against your neighbor." This commandment forbids lying, bribery, and forgery. It also bans any suggestion against the truth.* It forbids libel, slander, and backbiting, and calls for the truth and nothing but the truth. This also why the United States of America should and always will be a Judeo-Christian nation.

A further question that must be examined is who is charged with defending the Constitution after they leave office or retire. This is particularly crucial to military retirees. Each Trooper, Sailor, Airman, Marine, and Space Force member must honor their OATH. They can decide if there is a Threat! BUT only a Court of Law can determine if the Threat is Valid!

Can you Honestly and Truthfully say that you fully 100 percent believe that Rashida Talib, Omar Ilhan, Keith Ellison, or any other

Musim Appointed or Muslim Elected Officer of the Government is going to completely 100 percent support and defend the Constitution. It is for this reason Muslims should not be allowed to become Citizens, Vote, be Elected to or Appointed to any Elected or Appointed office.

Thus, this where the conflict between Islam and Constitution begins.

One question that needs to be answered right from the starting line is:" Is Islam a religion or a political organization? A religion is a free choice, you can join if you want to, you can leave if you so desire. It is a matter of CHOICE. A political system is not a matter of choice. It is a matter of law. You can be forced to join; you can be killed if you try to leave. You are on the whims of the state. Islam then is a political system as ruthless as North Korea. There is no choice in Islam, obey or die or lose a limb like for theft.

**This creates a conflict between the Constitution and Islam. It is due to the Islamic beliefs in Tawriya, Taqiyya, Kitman, Maruna, and Sharia. They hold that no oath to an infidel is binding. When the U.S. President meets an Islamic leader of a foreign country, like Turkey or Saudi Arabia, he is talking to a foreign ruler or head of state. Who is the Foreign Ruler talking to? First and Foremost, He is talking to an INFIDEL who is the head of an INFIDEL NATION. So, no treaty or pact is binding with an INFIDEL NATION. President Biden proved this when dealing with the Crown Prince of Saudi Arabia. [(https://www.npr.org/2022/06/25/1107628743/biden-will-visit-saudi-arabia-to-ask-for-an-increase-in-oil-production. )( https://nypost.com/2022/08/03/saudis-thumb-nose-at-bidens-request-to-boost-oil-output/)]. The Turkish Leader does not value a Pact or Treaty or Agreement with Israel, signed by the President of Turkey. He sees it as just a piece of paper since Israel is not a Moslem nation and according to the Koran, Jews are to be exterminated.**

So, what are Tawriya, Taqiyya, Kitman, Muruna?

Taqiyya - Saying something that is not true as it relates to Muslim identity (i.e., whether one is a Muslim or what being a Muslim means). This is a Shiite term: the Sunni counterpart is Muda 'rat.

Kitman - Lying by omission. Muslim apologists quote only a fragment of verse 5:32. It says, "if anyone kills, it shall be as if he had killed all mankind." They neglect to mention the rest of the verse and the next. They mandate murder for undefined cases of "corruption" and "mischief." Another form of kitman is to quote only the few peaceful passages from the Quran. They know that those were later abrogated by a more militant, contradictory verse. Here is an example: "There is no compulsion in religion" (Surah 2:256). "Are they seeking a religion other than Allah's? Every soul in the heavens and earth has submitted to Him, willingly or by compulsion." (Surah 3:83, Later Medina)

Tawriya - Creating a false impression by saying something true. It is done knowing the listener will misinterpret it. This practice has a broader application than taqiyya.

Muruna - 'Blending in' by setting aside or denying or hiding some practices of Islam or Sharia in order to advance others.

Scriptural References

Quran (16:106) - Establishes that there are circumstances that can "compel" a Muslim to tell a lie.

Quran (3:28) - This verse tells believers not to befriend non-Muslims, unless to "guard themselves" from danger. So, a Muslim may seem friendly to non-Muslims, but they should not feel friendly.

Quran (9:3) - "...Allah and His Messenger are free from liability to the idolaters..." The dissolution of oaths is with pagans who remained at Mecca following its capture. They did nothing wrong but were evicted anyway. (The next verse refers only to those who have a personal agreement with Muhammad as individuals - see Ibn Kathi vol 4, p 49)

Quran (66:2) - "Allah has already ordained for you the dissolution of your oaths..." Today's reader finds no specified circumstances for betraying your word. This leaves the verse open to interpretation. Yusuf Ali's commentary states: "If your vows prevent you from doing good, or making peace, you should expiate the vow." (Presumably, anything that advances Islam is 'doing good'.)

Quran (40:28) - A man is introduced as a believer, but one who had to "hide his faith" among those who are not believers.

Quran (2:225) - "Allah will not call you to account for thoughtlessness in your oaths, but for the intention in your hearts" (see also 5:89)

Quran (3:54) - "And they (the disbelievers) schemed, and Allah schemed (against them): and Allah is the best of schemers." The Arabic word used here for scheme (or plot) is makara, which means 'cunning,' 'guile' and 'deceit'. If Allah is supremely deceitful toward unbelievers, then there is little basis for denying that Muslims are allowed to do the same. (See also 8:30 and 10:21)

These verses are interpreted to mean that, sometimes, a Muslim may be "compelled" to deceive for a greater purpose.

Hadith and Sira

Sahih Bukhari (52:269) - "The Prophet said, 'War is deceit.'" This refers to the murder of User ibn Zarim and his thirty unarmed companions by Muhammad's men after they were "guaranteed" safe passage (see Additional Notes in the Bukhari).

Sahih Bukhari (49:857) - "He who makes peace between the people by inventing good information or saying good things, is not a liar." In other words, lying is permissible when the end justifies the means.

Sahih Bukhari (84:64-65) - Speaking from a position of power at the time, Ali confirms that lying is permitted in order to deceive an "enemy." The Quran defines the 'enemy' as "disbelievers" (4:101).

Sahih Muslim (32:6303) - "...he did not hear that exemption was granted in anything what the people speak as lie but in three cases: in battle, for bringing reconciliation amongst persons and the narration of the words of the husband to his wife, and the narration of the words of a wife to her husband (in a twisted form in order to bring reconciliation between them)."

Sahih Bukhari (50:369) - Recounts the murder of a poet, Ka'ba bin al-Ashraf, at Muhammad's insistence. The men who volunteered for the assassination used dishonesty to gain Ka'ba's trust, pretending that they had turned against Muhammad. This drew the victim out of his fortress, whereupon he was brutally slaughtered.

Though not called taqiyya, Muhammad used deception. He signed a 10-year treaty with the Meccans (known as Hudaibiya). It allowed him access to their city while he secretly prepared his forces for a takeover. The unsuspecting residents were easily conquered when he broke the treaty two years later. Some of the people in the city who had trusted him at his word were executed.

Another example of lying is when Muhammad used deception. He tricked his enemies into letting down their guard by pretending to seek peace. This happened in the case of Ka'b bin al-Ashraf (as noted). It later occurred against Usayr ibn Zarim, a surviving leader of the Banu Nadir tribe. The Muslims had evicted the Banu Nadir from their home in Medina.

At the time, Usayr ibn Zarim was trying to raise an army against the Muslims. He sought support from a tribe allied with the Quraish, whom Muhammad had already declared war on. Muhammad's "emissaries" went to ibn Zarim. They persuaded him to leave his safe haven to meet the prophet of Islam in Medina to discuss peace. Once vulnerable, the Muslims easily massacred the leader and his thirty companions. They were probably unarmed, having been promised safe passage (Ibn Ishaq 981, Ibn Kathir v.4 p.300).

Such was the reputation of early Muslims for lying and killing that even those who "accepted Islam" did not feel entirely safe. Consider the fate of Jadhima. When Muslim "missionaries" approached this tribe, one member insisted they would be slaughtered. They had already "converted" to Islam to avoid just such a fate. The others insisted they could trust the Muslim leader's promise. They would not be harmed if they offered no resistance. (After convincing the skeptic to lay down his arms, the unarmed men of the tribe were tied up and beheaded by the missionaries - Ibn Ishaq 834 & 837).

How can any Moslem be trusted? Their oaths to infidels are not binding. Thus, Muslims should not hold public office or even be citizens. They cannot be trusted to support the Constitution. As a final reminder remember this from Gatestone Institute( Yes, I am repeating myself, this is that critical for you to remember):

"I am not American," said the Islamist; "I am Muslim."

by Majid Rafizadeh December 2, 2017, at 5:00 am

For Islamists, non-Muslim land is different from Muslim land. Many can't identify with a Western land, flag, or nationality. They may have been born there, and their families lived there for generations.

Brainwashing people to reject their flag and nationality disrupts community ties and communication. It pits the indoctrinated person against the entire society and his own countrymen and develops an "us versus them" mentality.

This view brings with it a wish for waging jihad against one's birth country. It creates the priority -- if the country attacking it is ruled by shari'ah -- of joining the enemy to fight against one's birth country.

Several years ago, when first in the United States on a teaching scholarship, one issue leapt out. A man asked an innocent enough question: Where I was from? I told him; then, as a courtesy, asked him the same question.

"I am a Muslim," he smiled.

Thinking that perhaps he had not understood the question -- he sounded American or English -- I asked if he was from the United States.

"I am not American," he said again; "I am a Muslim."

I later learned he was an Islamist. He was a preacher of strict religious teachings. Many of his followers shared his views.

In Iran and Syria, where I was born and raised, I had never before heard this answer.

Later, while speaking in Europe, these notions kept resurfacing. Radical Islamists, particularly in Britain and France, proclaim themselves first to be Muslim. Even when they speak with English, French or American accents, they do not name their countries -- even to me, someone from the Middle East.

Their response signals a reason for concern in the countries they live in now. To begin with, for Islamists, non-Muslim land is different from Muslim land. Many cannot identify with a Western land, flag, or nationality. They may have been born there, and their families may have lived there for generations.

This view is far different from that in the Middle East.

One day, I asked an American imam why he did not identify himself as an American. Millions of people, I said to him, dream of coming to the US and becoming Americans; why would anyone want to reject this?

He quoted said one of the founding fathers of Islamist thoughts, Sayyid Qutb:

"The homeland of the Muslim is not a piece of land. It is what he defends. The Muslim's nationality is not a government-defined one. It is how he is identified. The Muslim's family is not just blood relations.

It is where he finds solace and what he defends. The Muslim's flag is not a country's flag. It is what he honors and under which he is martyred. The Muslim's victory is not a military one. It is what he celebrates and is thankful to God for.""

It became clear that Western Islamists were stricter than the Middle Eastern ones I had grown up with. Once, I mentioned a deceased imam in a casual chat with an American Islamist preacher and his followers. I forgot to add a religious praise to the name, like "Allah's peace be upon him."" There was a chill. The conversation came to a halt. The American Islamist preacher and his followers did not hesitate to express their anger.

You see that brainwashing people not to identify with a flag and a nationality disrupts community ties and communication. It pits the indoctrinated person against the entire society and his own countrymen and develops an "us versus them" mentality. The indoctrinated group then wants to create its own group. For Islamists, it is an ummah (borderless Islamic community). Emotion and sympathy for fellow countrymen vanish. People feel isolated and see themselves as separate from other citizens. Respect for the social order and the laws of the land vanish, as Islamic laws become more vital, and obedience is then just to shari'ah.

Islamist teachings in the West seem to aim at indoctrination. They want followers to identify with Islamist ideals, not a nationality. Also, Islamist beliefs should come before anything else, even family and friends.

The teachings of these Islamist preachers further echo what Sayed Qutb said:

"A Muslim has no relationship with his family except through [Allah]. They are also joined by blood." A Muslim has no country except where God's Shari'ah is upheld. Human ties must be based on a relationship with God. A Muslim has no nationality except his belief. It makes him part of the Muslim community in Dar-ul-Islam. A Muslim has no relatives except those who share his belief in God. This creates a bond with other Believers through their relationship with God."

Do these Western Islamists then ever identify themselves with their land and flag? Not, according to their teachings, until the law of the land is shari'ah. As Syed Qutb also stated:

"The fatherland is where the Islamic faith and way of life, and God's Shari'ah, prevail. Only this meaning of 'fatherland' is worthy of a human being." There is only one place on earth that is the home of Islam (Dar-ul-Islam). It is where an Islamic state is established, the Shari'ah is the authority, and God's limits are observed. All Muslims must administer the state's affairs with mutual consultation. The rest of the world is the home of hostility (Dar-ul-Harb). A Muslim can have only two possible relations with Dar-ul-Harb: peace with a contractual agreement, or war. A country with which there is a treaty will not be considered the home of Islam."

This view brings with it a wish for waging jihad (war in the cause of Islam) against one's birth country. It creates the priority -- if the country attacking it is ruled by shari'ah -- of joining the enemy to fight against one's birth country.

"The honor of martyrdom is achieved only when one is fighting in the cause of God, and if one is killed for any other purpose, this honor will not be attained."

Brainwashing people to reject a flag and a nationality harms community ties and communication. It pits the indoctrinated person against the entire society and his own countrymen and develops an "us versus them" mentality. Pictured: Muslims demonstrate in Sydney, Australia, September 15, 2012. (Image source: Jamie Kennedy/Flickr)

Western governments must address the rise of extreme Islamist beliefs. They have serious social, political, and security implications. These beliefs disrupt the social order, peace, and democracy. They harm human rights and security. If allowed to continue, these beliefs will become more rampant, and the consequences more severe.

Dr. Majid Rafizadeh is a business strategic advisor. He is a Harvard-educated scholar and a political scientist. He is also a board member of the Harvard International Review. He is the president of the International American Council on the Middle East. He is the author of "Peaceful Reformation in Iran's Islam". He can be reached at Dr.Rafizadeh@Post. Harvard.Edu.

Islam does not allow for equality between sexes or races. It supports slavery and does not believe in separating Church and State. Take Egypt, for example. The main legislative bodies are the constitutional court and parliament. But, al-Azhar is the de facto theocratic body. The constitution's second article states, "the principal source of legislation is Islamic Jurisprudence." This terror-indoctrinating institution and its madrassas get over 20 billion Egyptian pounds (over $1.2 billion) in annual government funding. For decades, the institution has pushed for heinous crimes and psychosexual disorders. It has also militarized Islam. So has **al-Mustafa** in Iran.

Now a second part of the problem is on a grand scale. If an Official deliberately lies to the public, they are undermining the Constitution. If the member is not REMOVED because of politics, the responsible District Attorney is doing the same and should be removed. The Fact that Schiff and Nadler are still in Office is only the tip of a HUGE iceberg. The only thing that matters in these trials is the answer to one question; DID YOU LIE IN OFFICE or TO CONGRESS or THE PUBLIC. IF the answer is yes, they should be removed and barred from holding public office. If a District Attorney chose not to prosecute, or to do so for political reasons, they should suffer the same fate. Their actions would not be for equal justice, but to serve a political agenda. No one who is removed should be allowed to collect a retirement. Also, a full audit of their fiscal history for insider trading should be done. I bet it has been hidden, like with Pelosi and Fauci.

When was the last time any member of Congress or the Executive Branch got removed and jailed for lying? Or betraying the Constitution. The District Attorney for OUR nation's capital, Washington, District of Columbia, must be asleep at the switch. Remember some of these lies have cost people dearly and worse, cost lives of the military, law enforcement, and worst of all, the innocent.

Just for the record, there is huge difference between not answering to the call of the truth and the Oath. In the course of my United States Navy career, I had the extreme pleasure to serve under and get to know Admiral Samuel Gravely. To make a point, once in a private conversation, I had asked a rather direct question. Admiral Gravely told me he would not lie to me and tell me he did not know the answer. What Gravely said next stuck with me. Admiral Gravely said "I do know your answer, I am not allowed to share it you." That is difference between lying to people and staying Honest. This made an indelible impression on me that lying is never a good solution. Unfortunately, many politicians never learn that lesson for a number of reasons. Top reasons are a political agenda, corruption, a lust for power, and a moral failure. These should be reason enough to resign. Of course, to a Politician, Honor means nothing, Power means everything. And the Truth has no Iron Rod to it.

If Congress, which cannot police itself, is unable to act, then the individual state governments must remove their Representatives for perjury: Swalwell, Schiff, Nadler, Omar, Tlaib, Waters, and Blumenthal. The States should consider overturning the Seventeenth Amendment. It would return control of the Senators to their state legislatures. This would make it easier to remove a bad or irresponsible Senator. Also, the states need to remove unfit Senators and Representatives, like Diane Feinstein, Joe Biden, Charles Schumer, John Fetterman, and Jerry Nadler. They are corruption cases waiting to happen, but they won't. They, unlike you, are protected.

Given that Moslems support slavery, child marriage, and pedophilia, and that they lie and favor "might makes right" and Sharia. They also tend to support the Democrat Party, which reciprocates, one conclusion follows. The Democrat Party is the ANTI-CONSTITUTION Party.

See the little dot? That is the final point. Remember, Muslims have been lying for over 1,390 years. They have honed their skills in it. If a Muslim deceives you, do not be surprised. The West does not learn anything from the history of the previous generations and is very gullible. This is why Muslims should NOT be allowed to hold any office. Islam views women and children as property. It supports slavery and Sharia. It rejects all infidel nations and their governments, like the Constitution. There is no equal rights. The Taliban banned Music and punished Music teachers and players. Muslims will kill gays, and trans. Finally Moslems support Pedophilia with marriage for girls at six, sex at nine, regardless of development. This country supports Muslims by allowing little girls to be taken from school and married in a foreign country. The U.S. then allows their "husbands" to join them here. There is no pact, treaty, or agreement that is safe between any infidel government. Moslems have had 1400 years of practice at lying. They break truces, pacts, and agreements with Infidels and see no reason to stop.

Currently, there is no standard of Equal Justice. There is no punishment for lying to the Public or Congress. Any punishment for a political person depends on the party in power. In short, **THERE IS NO STANDARD OF JUSTICE because "bearing False Witness is sanctioned or allowed.** This applies to Congress and some Executive Branch department heads. This includes Lois Lerner, Andrew McCabe (Note: Retirement is not punishment if it is a firing{ Congratulations, you are retired, I mean FIRED}), Hillary Clinton, Christopher Wray, the fifty who signed the Trump Collusion letter, and Alejandro Mayorkas as the Standard Bearer. Remember the very foundation of the Constitution is the Ninth Commandment. Without the Ninth Commandment, all the rest of the Constitution is meaningless. **This should not be!** This a reminder, You shall not bear false witness **Bible reference - Exodus 20:15: *"You shall not bear false witness against your neighbor."** This commandment forbids lying, bribery, and forgery. It also forbids any suggestion against the truth.* It forbids libel, slander, and backbiting, and calls for the truth and nothing but the truth. This also why the United States of America should and always will be a Judeo-Christian nation. Try to be worthy of our Constitution.

# Code Red Drill

Scenario Background: An explosion occurs at the checkpoint. The following are KIA:

Manager

Supervisors

Half or all of shift Senior personnel on station

Who orders Code Red?

What should you do before you bail, if you are a lead?

SSI

Duty phone

Duty Radio

TSOs on station-give direction.

What should you avoid?

PANIC!!!

Be aware of structural damage

Elevator-out of operation - Wheelchairs

Stairs-condition

Doorways-solid not warped

HazMat

X-ray machines – heavy metal – poisoning – beryllium for example

ETDs – heavy metal

After ten seconds a second explosion occurs in another terminal (announce to group)

Do you return to the checkpoint?   Yes, if trained          no if not trained otherwise stay clear (EMT/first aid)

How long do you wait before you return to the checkpoint?

smoke is grey-no fire-see through

If a lead, what do you start to do?

Report in – Phone is probably out – SO Messenger - Cellphone net overload.

Take command

Where do you look for bandage material? Stores

What about EMTs?

Tied up elsewhere at another explosion

How long do you work on wounded? Gut Instinct.

What might an explosion wound look like? Tears (shrapnel creates cuts and holes)

What are things that might need to be avoided?

Hazmat

Electrical cables

Pipes

Broken floating glass-divider for exit lane

Ceiling mounted electrical devices- air conditioner fans

Electrocution-Water plus Electricity

Buzzwords

Location-Do not say location if ears are involved, Buzzword = Discretion.

Type of threat

Fire/smoke

Hazmat

Oil

Electric Lines

Water

Number of bad guys

Number of casualties

Modify as needed/Example:  Charley Foxtrot Hotel Bravo Three India Six-Translation - Location Concourse "C" Fire Hazmat Bad guys 3 Injured - 6

Discretion: One Unified Buzzword/ Phrase on any Radio: Imaginary - Supervisor Thorvald Office Three – Supervisor- Imaginary – Supervisor/Office Three – Third Floor or Concourse C

Periodically Change – Once per year or six months.

The big four attacks

The biggest problem in a single word in ALL these attacks including FLL was "INTERFACE." There was no grand plan for interfacing with police or military units brought on the scene in the emergency. The first thing the "guests LEO/Military" had to do was find the "Host" or who was in charge and learn the battlefield. Then the first thing the bottom of the food chain had to learn was who were the guests and how the New Chain of Command works. At Beslan, three different commanders all claimed to be in charge. After the event was over, it became a game of three card Monty for avoiding blame. What is needed is a drill with a single command point for registration practice involving local forces, so people have some idea where to go before it happens with an alternate in case the primary site is involved or attacked. Preferably, the Alternate is near but not on the battlefield and should be a communications center.

1972 September 5/6 **Munich-Olympics** The **Munich massacre** was a terrorist attack carried out during the 1972 Summer Olympics in Munich, West Germany, by eight members of the Palestinian militant organization Black September, who infiltrated the Olympic Village, killed two members of the Israeli Olympic team, and took nine others hostage.[1][2][3][4] Black September called the operation «Iqrit and Biram[dubious – discuss]»,[5][6] after two Palestinian Christian villages whose inhabitants were expelled by the Israel Defense Forces (IDF) during the 1948 Arab–Israeli War.[7][8][9] The Black September commander was Luttif Afif, who was also their negotiator. West German neo-Nazis gave the group logistical assistance.[10]Shortly after the hostages were taken, Afif demanded the release of 234 Palestinian prisoners who were being held in Israeli jails, plus the West German–imprisoned founders of the Red Army Faction, Andreas Baader and Ulrike Meinhof.[11][12] West German police ambushed the terrorists, and killed five of the eight Black September members, but the rescue attempt failed and all of the hostages were killed.[13] A West German policeman was also killed in the crossfire, and **the West German government was criticized for the poor execution of its rescue attempt and its overall handling of the incident.** The three surviving perpetrators were Adnan Al-Gashey, Jamal Al-Gashey, and Mohammed Safady, who were arrested, only to be released the next month in the hostage exchange that followed the hijacking of Lufthansa Flight 615. By then, the Israeli government had launched an assassination campaign, which authorized Mossad to track down and kill anyone who had played a role in the attack.

2004 September 1 **Beslan School Siege** Russia First Day of School The **Beslan school siege** (also referred to as the **Beslan school hostage crisis** or the **Beslan massacre**)[2][3][4] was a rebel **It lasted three days,** an attack that started on 1 September 2004. **It lasted three days, and involved the imprisonment of more than 1,100 people as hostages, (including 777 children)**[5] **ending with the deaths of 334 people, 186 of them children,**[6] **as well as 31 of the attackers.**[1] It is considered the deadliest school shooting in history.[7]The crisis began when a group of armed terrorists occupied School Number One (SNO) in the town of Beslan, North Ossetia (an autonomous republic in the North Caucasus region of Russia) on 1 September 2004. The hostage-takers were members of the Riyad-us Saliheen, sent by the Chechen warlord Shamil Basayev, who demanded Russia withdraw from and recognize the independence of Chechnya. On the third day of the standoff, Russian security forces stormed the building.

2016 March 22 **Brussels Airport Attack** On 22 March 2016, two coordinated terrorist attacks in and close to Brussels, Belgium, were carried out by the Islamic State (IS). Two suicide bombers detonated bombs at Brussels Airport in Zaventem just outside Brussels, and one detonated a bomb on a train leaving Maelbeek/Maalbeek metro station in the European Quarter of Brussels. Thirty-two people were killed and more than 300 were injured. Three perpetrators also died. A third airport attacker fled the scene without detonating his bomb, which was later found in a search of the airport. A second metro attacker also fled, taking his bomb with him. The Islamic State claimed responsibility for the attacks. The perpetrators belonged to a terrorist cell that had been involved in the November 2015 Paris attacks and the attacks happened shortly after a series of police raids targeting the group.

2016 June 28 The **Istanbul Ataturk airport attack** occurred on June 28, 2016. It was a **gun and bomb attack** at Istanbul's Ataturk airport, resulting in **41 deaths** and **over 230 injuries**. Three attackers arrived in a taxi and began firing at the terminal entrance. After exchanging fire with police, they **blew themselves up**. Although early signs pointed to the so-called Islamic State, no group officially claimed responsibility[1]. This tragic event highlighted the vulnerability of the airport, which lacked thorough security checks for vehicles entering the terminal. Since then, security measures have been reinforced to prevent such attacks. ☒

Learn more 1. bbc.com  2. en.wikipedia.org 3. yahoo.com

What were the motives behind this attack?

How did it impact airport security worldwide?

Are there any memorials for the victims?

Istanbul Ataturk airport attack: 41 dead and more than 230 hurt

https://www.bbc.com/news/world-europe-36658187

Two more

**2024 June 23**   On 23 June 2024, coordinated attacks were launched in the cities of Derbent and Makhachkala in the Russian republic of Dagestan in the North Caucasus.[4][5] Two synagogues, two Eastern Orthodox churches, and a traffic police post were attacked simultaneously[6][7] with automatic weapons and Molotov cocktails.[8] It was reported that 17 police officers and five civilians were killed[9] along with all five attackers.[10] The fatalities included a priest, Nikolay Kotelnikov.[11][12] The Kele-Numaz Synagogue was nearly completely destroyed by fire in the attack. Russian authorities designated the attack as an act of terrorism.[13] Russian media reported that five of the perpetrators were identified by authorities, including one son and two nephews of Magomed Omarov, the head of Dagestan›s Sergokalinsky District.[14][15][16] Omarov later submitted a resignation letter and was detained for questioning.[17] One of the attackers was a former president of the Sergokala section of the A Just Russia – For Truth Party.

2017 January 6 a **mass shooting** occurred at **Fort Lauderdale–Hollywood International Airport** in Broward County, Florida, United States, near the baggage claim in Terminal 2. Five people were killed while six others were injured in the shooting. About 36 people sustained injuries in the ensuing panic. Realizing checkpoint is not the only target. (Personal note: It was an unmitigated Disaster. If I was looking for a target, Fort Lauderdale would have been it. Letting people on to the Runway, put them in a clear Field of Fire with no cover anywhere. )

Training
Have a blank floor plan of the checkpoint Floor.
On the floor plan from memory mark
Exits
Fire extinguishers
First Aid kits
Dead End Passages
Hiding spots
Crucial Centers-Phone, Water, Electric, Etc. Varies in Room.
Drills
Arbitrary group of the workforce at random
Play survivors
Who is in charge?
Who is given injury?
How do you handle injured survivors or threats?
Evaluate response
Find your Alfa and Betas-train them
Get the Security Center to put a bullet proof block around the Supervisor and in case of a multiple prong attack ties up EMS.
Deputy Stations
First Aid training
Take lessons home, if caught in an incident away from job, family will know how to react or what do.
Make sure the bottom of the Food Chain is TOTALLYBRIEFED So as know what is expected of them. In private security, I attended several management tabletop discussions, when I asked who briefed the troops, there was none planned. Policy changed.

Remember "Two Up, Two Down". Learn the basics of your Supervisor's Supervisor Job, and train two down for same reason, Casualties

Remember **an incident may last more than one day if hostages**.
Remember Terrorist are lazy.
Evacuation
Do not be at the front so you are driven into an ambush
Do not be at the back so terrorist can catch up with you'
Be on the side so you can peel off if you find an open door but know your terrain and hallways.
Hide high or very low, field of vision. The closer the Terrorist is the better your chance of being outside the field of vision.,

Above All be Honest in your assessment. If you are not **aware** of your battlefield, you are a target waiting to happen. Ban people walking around on Cell Phones because they are unaware. Cellphone=Stationary Target or Hostage waiting to happen, but more aware than a moving target. If on the phone, notice what is going on around you.

The videos are for weapon/bag awareness at checkpoint.
Videos
Concealed knives
www.youtube.com/watch?v=UVVtgDJ--W0
Concealed Guns
www.youtube.com/shorts/hKgB2GU3oOU
www.youtube.com/watch?v=fwetWJN6AU8&t=56s
www.youtube.com/watch?v=hLS6CZZmw30

# A Prepper's Advice: How To Survive A Mass Shooting

August 5, 2019 Featured, Life Stories Authored by Daisy Luther via The Organic Prepper blog,

Mass shootings are happening more and more often in America. Yesterday, there were two mass shootings within 24 hours that claimed the lives of 29 people and injured 52 more. A mass z hellish nightmare you wouldn't wish on your worst enemy.

A synopsis of the event came from a Facebook live video. (Is it just me or do you find it strange that someone was recording a video and not running like hell?)

At the start of the video, a woman runs toward the store, past a truck that a shopping cart has run into, with a body lying on the ground beside it.

Children were holding a fundraiser at the store and some reportedly were among the casualties.

At the front of the store, victims' bodies are shown near a table that appeared to have items for sale. The body of a man in blue jeans and a blue shirt is seen on the ground near the table, lying on his stomach, seemingly dead, as a woman rushes over to help. Near him is a woman, taking cover between a garbage can and the wall.

A person is shown lying motionless to the left of the table, under a shade covering set up over it, as a woman tries to help. Nearby, by the wall of the building, a man lies on his side in a pool of dark blood, with a bandage on his back.

A voice tells him, "Try not to move," adding, "Stay with me, OK?"

Wailing is heard in the background, as people tend to others lying injured nearby. *(source)*

**You have to know what to do before an event like this occurs.**

One factor that allows shooters to get so many victims is that most folks don't know what to do in such an event. Most people don't think ahead when they're going to Wal-Mart or enjoying an evening in a popular pedestrian area.

But these days, a person has to have a plan anywhere they go, it seems. And they also have to have a survival mindset, practicing the 3 steps of survival repeatedly until it becomes completely natural for them.

If you are in the first wave of victims, that's just bad luck, and there isn't much you can do about that. But if you are not in that first wave, then you have a chance to take action and survive. But you have to know what to do and be able to take those life-saving actions.

**What is *not* important if you find yourself in the midst of a shooting**

This is an unpopular opinion, but here goes.

**Strictly from a survival point of view, it doesn't matter who it is doing the shooting or whether it's a "false flag."** If you were there, it won't help you to know who did the 9/11 attacks or the bombings in Boston, London, and Paris. It doesn't matter whether the shooting at Sandy Hook was perpetrated by a kid with behavioral issues or by operatives with an agenda. It doesn't matter that the guy shooting up a Walmart in Texas wrote an anti-Hispanic manifesto.

If your focus is preparedness and survival, the most important thing you can be doing right now is learning from horrific events.

No matter who you believe, the key lesson is survival. Muslim extremists, a Hispanic hater, or a woman-hater who can't get a date. Some say it was a state-sponsored act to take away our freedoms.

This article is not a debate about the different conspiracy theories. If you are present during a terror attack, my opinions on the culprit don't matter and neither do yours. <u>All that matters in those minutes or hours is surviving</u>.

Let's not debate how these two shootings in 24 hours let the 2020 candidates tug at the heartstrings for gun control. What matters is whether you can survive in such a scenario.

**Here are the things you need to do before a shooting ever happens.**

First things first, even when you're there for fun, you must be paying attention. You should always scan an area for exits and potential cover. You should pay attention to the people around you. Know the baseline behavior of your setting. It will help you notice anything unusual. Let me explain this further.

We can maintain a high level of situational awareness merely by being observant. One way to develop your skills is to play something called Kim's Game. My friend Scott, at Graywolf Survival, <u>used to use the game to train his soldiers in situational awareness</u>. He wrote:

*Situational awareness is key to knowing your environment. It helps you understand your circumstances and options. There are many examples, but would you notice the printing of someone's ankle from a concealed weapon if you had to follow him to barter for goods? Would you remember enough details of the turn of a path you passed two hours ago to be able to find it again? If you were attacked, would you be able to give a good enough description of the subject and getaway vehicle to have him identified?*

Kim's Game comes from a novel by Rudyard Kipling and is something you can play with your family, anywhere, anytime. Go HERE to learn more about how to play it.

A higher level of situational awareness can help you in many ways, should you be unfortunate enough to be present during a mass shooting.

It can help by:

Allowing you to identify a threat before it becomes active

Allowing you to locate exits and routes to the exits

Allowing you to determine sources of cover

If you can spot a threat before it exists, you can sometimes prevent an attack. At the very least, you can better protect yourself and your family. A book by Patrick Van Horne and Jason A. Riley describes this as being on the "left of bang". The left of bang describes the moments before something bad happens. It's when you sense something is wrong but can't identify it.

The book, Left of Bang: How the Marine Corps' Combat Hunter Program Can Save Your Life, discusses how establishing a baseline can help you to identify a threat. (I can't recommend this book strongly enough.)

A baseline is a "normal" for your immediate environment. Once you have a baseline for behavior in a specific environment, then it's easier to spot anomalies. According to Left of Bang, it's the anomalies that should put you on high alert. *"Anomalies are things that either do not happen and should or that do happen and shouldn't."*

The earlier you're aware that something is going down, the better your chances are of survival.

**Know what gunfire sounds like.**

A lot of people who were interviewed after the Walmart shooting said that when they first heard the shots, they didn't realize what it was. They thought it was noise from construction or boxes being dropped. For a few seconds, people were frozen, trying to grasp what was happening. During an event like this, a pause of a few seconds could mean the difference between life and death. The faster you take action the more likely you are to survive.

**Always have a plan.**

We can't foresee all eventualities, like this one, for example, but it helps to always have a survival mindset. It has long been a game with my kids (yeah, we're a strange family) to identify exits and potential weapons if we sit down to eat at a restaurant or go to the movies. Something we focused on in Selco's Urban Survival Course in Croatia was finding alternative exits in a mall, locating cover, and finding everyday items that could be used as weapons.

Knowing where to go without having to look for it in the heat of the moment will save time that could be spent acting. We also look for sources of cover.

**Understand the difference between cover vs. concealment.**

Every NRA course I've taken discusses the difference between cover and concealment. If you must use your firearm, someone may be ready to shoot back. Concealment is enough to hide you but not enough to protect you from bullets. Cover is something sturdy enough to stop a bullet. Examples are a concrete road divider, a car's engine block, a refrigerator, a steel door, and a brick wall.

The video of the Las Vegas shooting showed many seeking cover behind flimsy barriers. They are not enough to protect you from a high-powered gun and a shooter spraying an area.

**Separate from the crowd.**

In a mass shooting, the shooter aims to kill as many as possible. So, he'll likely aim at the crowd instead of picking off those who moved away from it.

One possible strategy would be, then, to get away from the crowd. You and your group would be less alluring than a hundred panicked people huddled together for maximum harm.

**Don't get down or play dead.**

Lots of people crouched down and got as low as they could. In many situations, this would be the best bet, but not this one. The person was shooting from up high, aiming downward. Being still and crouching down wouldn't do much to protect you from a person firing from this angle, nor would playing dead.

Action is nearly always a better choice than inaction. As well, getting down would make it more likely that you'd be trampled by a panicked crowd of people trying to get away from the area. After the Las Vegas shooting, Clark County Fire Chief Greg Cassell said a "wide range" of injuries included people trampled by the panicked crowds.

**Listen for reload.**

In a situation like this, there will be pauses in the shooting when the person stops to either reload or change firearms. That is your opportunity to make a dash for the exits or to take down the attacker. Don't wait too long to make your move, because it only takes an experienced gunman a few seconds to reload a familiar gun and then your chance is gone.

**There are only 3 courses of action.**

Sometimes regardless of how alert and observant we are, we can't predict when an attack is about to happen. There might be no indications in your immediate surroundings to alert yourself to the fact that something is going down. You may be blithely unaware until the moment that a perpetrator starts firing.

If you find yourself suddenly in the midst of a mass shooting, your actions should be one of the following:

1) ***Escape.*** *Get as far away from the threat as possible. This is where your early observant behavior comes in handy because you'll already know the escape routes. If you are in charge of vulnerable individuals like children, your first choice of actions should be to get them to safety if at all possible.*

2) ***Take cover.*** *If you can't get away, get behind something solid and wait for your opportunity to either escape or fight back. This is something else you may have observed when doing your earlier reconnaissance.*

3) ***Take out the threat.*** *If you are armed (and I really hope you are) and/or trained, use your abilities to help remove the threat. But know that sometimes you can't get a clear shot without putting other people at risk. Understand the power of your firearm and ammunition – will your bullet go through the perpetrator*

**The most important thing to consider here is not necessarily *which* action you will take. It's that you *will* take an action, not just stand there in shock. You can be a victim or you can be a warrior.** Unfortunately, modern life has made our survival instincts obsolete. But, you can overcome this with practice and study.

Keep in mind that fighting back doesn't always mean a fancy Krav Maga move that takes down two armed men with one trick maneuver. There are many ways to fight back, and not all of them require physical prowess. Don't let fear incapacitate you. Your brain is a weapon too.

Are you going to wait for someone to save you or are you going to save yourself? Don't be a kamikaze, but look for your opportunity.

And there comes a point in some of these situations in which survival is unlikely. ***Don't go down without a fight.***

## Final Thought

Is Islam a Religion or a Political Organization? It must be one or the other. Remember two things. First all Religion are voluntary, Islam is not. Second. ALL Religions condemn genocide. Islam endorses Genocide of any group not of their particular sects under the title unbeliever or infidel. Third, no Religion has somebody born just so some other group can kill them.

Fourth, in Modern times, Islam supports Slavery still. For reference, check the Egyptian Constitution and the phrase that "which your right-hand posses." For that reason, Islam sees women as Door Prizes in War.

If you have a single Mosque, you have a terrorism breeding ground. Remember there are all sorts of Jihadi Groups and Personnel, from little Children to teenagers to families to the Elderly, BUT there is only ONE A SINGLE "ANNIHILATE ALL INFIDELS AND THEIR SOCIETIES" QURAN. Stay alert!

# Intell Sources  29 August 2024

Topics
News

| | | | |
|---|---|---|---|
| 1. | **\*Newsletter** | | **\*https://www.gatestoneinstitute.org/** |
| 2. | **\*News\*** | **Robert Spencer** | **https://www.jihadwatch.org/** |
| 3. | **\*News\*** | **Pamela Gellar** | **https://gellerreport.com/** |
| 4. | **\*News Video\*** | **https://www.memri.org/tv** | |
| 5. | **\*News\*** | **https://www.counterextremism.com** | |
| 6. | *\*News China\** | **https://www.scmp.com/news** | *South China Sea* |
| 7. | **\*News China\*** | **https://experts.scmp.com/latest-news** | |
| 8. | **\*News** | https://www.analyzingamerica.org/ | |
| 9. | \*News | http://www.imgclients.com/ic/site/hotspots | |
| 10. | \*News | https://www.investigativeproject.org/ | |
| 11. | News \$\$\$ | https://www.trackingterrorism.org/ | |
| 12. | News | https://www.intelcenter.com/ | |
| 13. | **News** | **https://www.meforum.org/** | |
| 14. | **\*News** | **https://www.africaintelligence.com/** | |
| 15. | News \$\$\$ | https://thefederalist.com/ | |
| 16. | Left News | https://theintercept.com | |
| 17. | \*News\* | https://www.politico.com/ | |
| 18. | News | https://www.govexec.com | Government Executive |

Authors

| | | | |
|---|---|---|---|
| 19. | Author/ | Bridget Gabriel | https://www.actforamerica.org/ |
| 20. | Author/ FGM | Ayaan Ali Hirsi | https://www.theahafoundation.org/ |
| 21. | Author | Wafa Sultan | http://wafasultan.blogspot.com |
| 22. | **Author** | **Raymond Ibrahim** | **http://www.raymondibrahim.com/** |
| 23. | Author | Daniel Pipes | http://www.danielpipes.org/ |

## Research

24. **Research**       **https://www.hudson.org/**
25. *News       http://www.imgclients.com/ic/site/hotspots
26. *News       Most Wanted Fugitives - Florida Department of Highway       Safety and Motor Vehicles (flhsmv.gov)
27. *News*       http://www.targetofopportunity.com/palestinian_truth.htm
28. News $$$       https://www.stratfor.com/       Subscriber
29. Leftwing research       https://www.globalresearch.ca/
30. Research       https://brownstone.org/articles
31. Research       https://www.brookings.edu/       B r o o k i n g s Institute
32. **Energy News**       **https://www.energyintel.com/**       **EVs vs Petrol**
33. Think Tank       https://www.csis.org/       Center for Strategic and International Studies

## Countries

34. **News**     **Japan**     **http://the-japan-news.com/news/business**
35. **News**     **Arab**     **http://www.arabnews.com/**
36. **News**     **Iran**     **http://en.farsnews.com/**
37. **News**     **Germany**     **https://www.dw.com/en**
38. **News**     **Denmark**     **https://www.thelocal.dk**
39. **News**     **https://www.indiandefensenews.in**     *India Defense*
40. *News*     **https://defence.pk**     *Pakistan Defense*
41. **\*News Australia\***     **https://www.skynews.com.au/**
42. News Israel/World     https://jcpa.org/
43. Argentina     https://www.batimes.com.ar
44. Israel     https://www.jns.org/
45. Canada     https://www.youtube.com/@theplebreporter/featured
46. Egypt     https://english.aham.org.eg
47. India     https://www.theweek.in/
48. **Turkey**     **https://turkeypurge.com/**
49. Japan/Asia     https://asia.nikkei.com/
50. **Turkey**     **https://www.aa.com.tr/en**
51. **Russia**     **https://www.themoscowtimes.com/**
52. Russia     https://www.rbth.com/history/
53. North Korea     https://pscore.org/home/     Defectors
54. India (Hindi)     https://www.indiatoday.in/world/     **Learn**
55. **Middle East**     **https://www.middleeastmonitor.com**
56. **South America**     **https://www.world-newspapers.com/countries/ south-america**
57. Cities     https://www.city-journal.org/

58. Middle East          https://www.al-monitor.com

## Medical
59. *Medical     https://www.medpagetoday.com
60. Medical     https://www.medicinenet.com
61. ***Medical     https://www.ehstoday.com/          emergency health systems**
62. Health     https://www.healthline.com/
63. NIH          https://nihrecord.nih.gov/past-issues
64. Children's Health     https://childrenshealthdefense.org/defender/
65. Ear buds  https://soundunify.com/side-effects-of-headphones-on-the-brain/
66. ***Medical     https://interestingengineering.com          Medical/ anything else computer car etc.     CUTTING EDGE**

## Science
67. SCIENCE          https://cosmosmagazine.com          from     Australia science
68. ***Earthquake https://earthquake.usgs.gov/earthquakes/map     Volcanos**
69. ***Tropical Storms     https://www.tropicaltidbits.com**
70. Tropical Storms     https://www.wunderground.com/hurricane
71. **Tropical Storms     https://www.nhc.noaa.gov**
72. Weather Local     https://www.weather.gov
73. **Solar Storms     https://spaceweather.com/**
74. Genetics     https://geneticliteracyproject.org/
75. Darwin     https://www.discovery.org/          Store-AI, Darwin, ETC
76. Geoengineering     https://zerogeoengineering.com/
77. Seacology     https://www.seacology.org

## Economics
78. ***Finance*     https://mises.org/wire**
79. Economics     https://fee.org/     Foundation for Economic Education
80. Academic journal library     https://www.jstor.org/     Economics

## MILITARY
81. **Maritime News     https://gcaptain.com**
82. Military News:     Navy     Times= https://www.navytimes.com/
   • https://www.armytimes.com/          https://www.airforcetimes.com/
   • https://www.marinecorpstimes.com  https://www.militarytimes.com/
83. **Intell Lasers     MisterrRobots.com          Maui Fires**

84. **Intell Lasers Stevevavis.com** **Maui Fires**
85. **Biowarfare  https://www.ncbi.nlm.nih.gov/pmc/articles/PMC1326439/ Israel**
86. **Biowarfare  h t t p s : / / w w w . d w . c o m / e n / covid-vaccines-as-passive-biological-warfare-in-middle-east/a-56471435**
87. NATO  https://www.nato.int/cps/en/natohq/news.htm
88. Intell  http://www.sofx.com  SpecialOperations
   Forces
   Newsletter
89. Persecution
90. Persecution  https://www.intoleranceagainstchristians.eu
91. Persecution  h t t p s : / / e c l j . o r g / r e l i g i o u s - f r e e d o m / u n / the-label-christianophobia-in-human-rights-law

*-used regularly  $-subscribe versus free

New
1. UN monitor  UNwatch.org
2. **Survival Planning**  **https://tipsforsurvivalists.com**
3. **News**  **https://americascivilwarrising.org/**
4. Politics vs reality  https://wentworthreport.com
5. Research  https://www.wiley.com/en-us
6. Germany  https://qantara.de/en

www.ingramcontent.com/pod-product-compliance
Lightning Source LLC
Chambersburg PA
CBHW020439130626
46549CB00001B/217